DICTIONARY OF CONTRACT AND LEGAL TERMS FOR MANAGERS AND ENGINEERS

DICTIONARY
OF
CONTRACT AND LEGAL TERMS
FOR
MANAGERS AND ENGINEERS

By

SYED ALI DILAWER

BE, MBA, PMP, CCC, MRICS, ACIARB, MICA, GMP
Senior Project Control and Claims Consultant
Built Asset Consultancy
Abu Dhabi, UAE

UNIVERSITY SCIENCE PRESS

(An Imprint of Laxmi Publications Pvt. Ltd.)

BANGALORE • CHENNAI • COCHIN • GUWAHATI • HYDERABAD
JALANDHAR • KOLKATA • LUCKNOW • MUMBAI • RANCHI
NEW DELHI • BOSTON, USA

Published by :

UNIVERSITY SCIENCE PRESS

(An Imprint of Laxmi Publications Pvt. Ltd.)

113, Golden House, Daryaganj,
New Delhi-110002

Phone : 011-43 53 25 00
Fax : 011-43 53 25 28

www.laxmipublications.com
info@laxmipublications.com

First Edition : 2014

OFFICES

✆ **Bangalore**	080-26 61 15 61	✆ **Jalandhar**	0181-222 12 72
✆ **Chennai**	044-24 34 47 26	✆ **Kolkata**	033-22 27 37 73
✆ **Cochin**	0484-237 70 04, 405 13 03	✆ **Lucknow**	0522-220 95 78
✆ **Guwahati**	0361-254 36 69, 251 38 81	✆ **Mumbai**	022-24 91 54 15, 24 92 78 69
✆ **Hyderabad**	040-24 65 23 33	✆ **Ranchi**	0651-221 47 64

UDC-9698-095-DIC CONT LEGAL TERM MAN-DIL C—

Typeset at : Goswami Associates, Delhi.

Printed at: Repro Knowledgecast Limited, Thane

I would like to dedicate
this work to my daughter
Fatima

Preface

This Dictionary improves the ability of Managers and Engineers to communicate with and instruct legal and contracts personnel. You can achieve far better negotiated results if you have a good understanding of what contracts and their terminology actually mean. This will empower you to utilise your legal advice for specialist legal issues rather than strategic decision-making, over which you must have full control. It contains key words used in the day-to-day practice. If you are looking for definition of contract and legal terms, you will find them all arranged alphabetically in this valuable desk.

This Dictionary defines contracts and legal terms in easily understood English. In some cases, it gives an example of a situation to which the contract and legal term might apply in order to help illustrate the meaning. It would be a very useful addition to anyone's reference library. This Dictionary is a comprehensive source of meanings and use for thousands of today's most common contract and legal terms. Contract and Legal terms are presented in this Dictionary in a way that it should be understood by all.

This Dictionary is also useful for those without a qualification in law who nevertheless require some legal knowledge in the course of their work.

I believe that a copy of this book should be a part of every non-legal professional's toolkit, not just for reference, but also for the wealth of knowledge that it contains–all from respected sources.

Importance of each individual depends upon the ability and expertise which he or she has attained and capable of displaying.

–Author

CONTENTS

Chapter 1 CONTRACT

1.1 INTRODUCTION

A Contract is an agreement enforceable at law, made between two or more persons, by which rights are acquired by one or more for acts or forbearances on the part of the other(s).

The law is there to assist if the parties do not fulfil the duties they have voluntarily undertaken.

Construction contracts are fundamentally different from major service contracts. There are various types of construction contracts. The choice of contract depends on the basis of pricing and the contract strategy that best meets the project objectives. These are various in types and offer different ways of handling pricing, risk transfer, responsibility for performance, cost certainty, and complexity.

1.2 REQUIREMENT OF A VALID CONTRACT

A contract requires three things: an offer, acceptance, and consideration. That means that the Contractor / Supplier will offer to do the job for a certain price to you will accept that offer, and both of you get something out of the deal (you get the work, the contractor gets the money). Lacking anyone of those, what is written on paper but not a contract, and nobody is bound to it.

Essential Elements of a Valid Contract

- Proposal and acceptance
- Consideration—lawful consideration with a lawful object
- Capacity of parties to contract—competent parties
- Free Consent
- An agreement must not be expressly declared to be void

- Writing and registration if so required by law
- Certainty
- Possibility of performance
- Enforceable by law

1.3 CONTRACT DOCUMENTS

- The Contract Agreement
- The Tender
- The Letter of Acceptance
- The Conditions of Contract
- **Specifications:** Define the quality of the work to be executed
- **Drawings:** Define the scope of the work to be carried out
- **Bill of Quantities:** Define how the Contractor is to be paid

1.4 PARTIES INVOLVED IN THE CONTRACT

- The Employer
- The Financer
- The Designer(s)
- The Contractor(s)
- Management Consultants
- The Subcontractor(s)
- The Supplier(s)
- The Engineer
- The Adjudicator(s)

1.5 TYPES OF CONTRACT

Common types of contract are used in the engineering and construction industry

- Lump Sum Contract
- Unit Price Contract
- Cost Plus Contract
- Incentive Contracts
- Percentage of Construction Fee Contracts

1.5.1 Lump Sum Contract

A lump sum, sometimes called stipulated sum, contract is the most basic form of agreement between a supplier of services and a customer. The supplier agrees to provide specified services for a specific price. The receiver agrees to pay the price upon completion of the work or according to a negotiated payment schedule. In developing a lump sum bid, the builder will estimate the costs of labor and materials and add to it a standard amount for overhead and the desired amount of profit. Most builders will estimate profit and overhead to total about 12–16 percent of the project cost. This amount may be increased based on the builder's assessment of risk. If the actual costs of labor and materials are higher than the builder's estimate, the profit will be reduced. If the actual costs are lower, the builder gets more profit. Either way, the cost to the owner is the same. In practice, however, costs that exceed the estimates may lead to disputes over the scope of work or attempts to substitute less expensive materials for those specified.

1.5.2 Unit Price Contract

In a unit price contract, the work to be performed is broken into various parts, usually by construction trade, and a fixed price is established for each unit of work. For example, painting is typically done on a square foot basis. Unit price contracts are seldom used for an entire major construction project, but they are frequently used for agreements with sub-contractors. They are also often used for maintenance and repair work. In a unit price contract, like a lump sum contract, the contractor is paid the agreed upon price, regardless of the actual cost to do the work.

1.5.3 Cost Plus Contract

Contract agreement wherein the purchaser agrees to pay the cost of all labor and materials plus an amount for contractor overhead and profit (usually as a percentage of the labor and material cost).The contracts may be specified as:

Cost + Fixed Percentage Contract

For certain types of construction involving new technology or extremely pressing needs, the owner is sometimes forced to assume all risks of cost overruns. The contractor will receive the actual direct job cost plus a fixed percentage, and have little incentive to reduce job cost. Furthermore, if there are needs to complete the project, overtime payments to workers are common and will further increase the job cost. Unless there are compelling reasons, such as the urgency in the construction of military installations, the owner should not use this type of contract.

Cost + Fixed Fee Contract

Under this type of contract, the contractor will receive the actual direct job cost plus a fixed fee, and will have some incentive to complete the job quickly since its fee is fixed regardless of the duration of the project. However, the owner still assumes the risks of direct job cost overrun while the contractor may risk the erosion of its profits if the project is dragged on beyond the expected time.

- Cost + Fixed Fee with Guaranteed Maximum Price Contract

- Cost + Fixed Fee with Bonus Contract
- Cost + Fixed Fee with Guaranteed Maximum Price and Bonus Contract
- Cost + Fixed Fee with Agreement for Sharing Any Cost Savings Contract

These types of contracts are favored where the scope of the work is indeterminate or highly uncertain and the kinds of labor, material and equipment needed are also uncertain. Under this arrangement complete records of all time and materials spent by the contractor on the work must be maintained.

1.5.4 Incentive Contract

Compensation is based on the engineering and/or contracting performance according an agreed target-budget, schedule and/or quality.

The two basic categories of incentive contracts are:

Fixed Price Incentive Contract

Fixed Price Incentive Contracts are preferred when contract costs and performance requirements are reasonably certain.

Cost Reimbursement Incentive Contract

Cost Reimbursement Contract provides the initially negotiated fee to be adjusted later by a formula based on the relationship of total allowable costs to total target costs. This type of contract specifies a target cost, a target fee, minimum and maximum fees, and a fee adjustment formula. After project performance, the fee payable to the contractor is determined in accordance with the formula.

1.5.5 Percentage of Construction Fee Contract

Common for engineering contracts compensation is based on a percentage of the construction costs.

Chapter 2

STANDARDS FORM OF CONTRACTS

2.1 INTRODUCTION

Standard Form of Contracts are agreements that employ standardized, non-negotiated provisions, usually in pre-printed forms. These are sometimes referred to as "boilerplate contracts," "contracts of adhesion," or "take it or leave it" contracts. The terms, often portrayed in fine print, are drafted by or on behalf of one party to the transaction – the party with superior bargaining power who routinely engages in such transactions. With few exceptions, the terms are not negotiable by the consumer.

Standard form, business-to-consumer contracts fulfill an important efficiency role in the mass distribution of goods and services. These contracts have the potential to reduce transaction costs by eliminating the need to negotiate the many details of a contract for each instance a product is sold or a service is used. However, these contracts also have the ability to trick or abuse consumers because of the unequal bargaining power between the parties. For example, where a standard form contract is entered into between an ordinary consumer and the salesperson of a multinational corporation, the consumer typically is in no position to negotiate the standard terms; indeed, the company's representative often does not have the authority to alter the terms, even if either side to the transaction were capable of understanding all the terms in the fine print. These contracts are typically drafted by corporate lawyers far away from where the underlying consumer and vendor transaction takes place.

The danger of accepting unfair or unconscionable terms is greatest where these artful drafters of such contracts present consumers with attractive terms on the visible or "shopped" terms of most interest to consumers, such as price and quality, but then slip one-sided terms benefiting the seller into the less visible, fine print clauses least likely to be read or understood by consumers. In many cases, the consumer may not even see these contracts until the transaction has occurred. In some cases, the seller knows and takes advantage of the knowledge that consumers will not read or make decisions on these unfair terms.

2.2 ADVANTAGES

- Save time by using a standard form contract in your next business transaction. Pull out a preprinted contract and fill in the blanks. You can use this for real estate transactions, such as a rental agreement, where both parties agree on the basics of the contract and most of the terms. Fill in the length of the rental, the amount of the rent, and have both parties sign for a valid standard contract.
- Purchase a standard form contract normally used in your business. Find them at a stationary stores or office supply stores. Copy the standard form contract and file the copies to have them available each time you need them. Consider a software program which contains the standard form contract with fill able forms. Give your standard form contract a more professional look by inserting the names and addresses of the parties, as well as the terms directly into the contract before it is printed.
- Reduce time you may spend negotiating each of the terms of the standard form contract. Determine which terms are necessary for a smooth business transaction and concentrate your negotiation on those terms. Cross out the terms which are inapplicable and write in other applicable terms not covered in the standard form. Review terms such as arbitration or availability of attorney fees for dispute clauses, application of state laws clauses, and termination clauses to determine if these terms are acceptable.
- You can eliminate attorney fees with a standard form contract. Remove the need to have the attorney negotiate the contract, write the contract, and review the contract. Benefit with additional money in your pocket by using a standard contract to complete your business transaction.

2.3 DISADVANTAGES

- The forms are cumbersome, complex and often difficult to understand.
- Because the resulting contract is often a compromise, they are resistant to change. Much-needed changes take a long time to bring into effect.

2.4 TYPES OF STANDARD FORM OF CONTRACT

2.4.1 Introduction

This chapter listed prominent bodies and the standardized documents they offer related with different industries. The websites from which you may access documents are stated in particular sections.

2.4.2 Fédération Internationale des Ingénieurs-Conseils (FIDIC)

Introduction

The FIDIC suite of contracts

The FIDIC suite of construction contracts is written and published by the International Federation of Consulting Engineers. The FIDIC acronym stands for the French version of the Federation's name (Federation Internationale des Ingenieurs-Conseil).

The best known of the FIDIC contracts are the Red Book (building and engineering works designed by the Employer) and the Yellow Book (M and E, building and engineering works designed by the Contractor). The original edition of the Red Book dates back to 1957.

In recent years FIDIC has published many new contracts to complement the suite. The first of the new contracts was the Orange Book for design, build and turnkey works published in 1995.

In 1999 FIDIC published a revised suite of contracts with updated versions of the Red and Yellow books together with a Green Book as the short form of contract and a Silver Book for turnkey contracts.

More recently in 2005 FIDIC published an amended version of the Red Book for use by Multilateral Development Banks and in 2007 published a seminar edition of the Gold Book for Design, Build and Operate contracts.

Less well know FIDIC contracts are also available such as the Turquoise Book for Dredging and Reclamation Works published in January 2006 and the White Book model services agreement published in October 2006.

The FIDIC suite of contracts now covers a widerange of projects and methods of procurement. It is therefore likely that any international contractor or consultant working outside of the UK will frequently encounter FIDIC conditions of contract.

Sub-contractors will similarly encounter FIDIC derived conditions of contract where they are operating internationally. Even subcontractors that only operate within a particular country will from time to time encounter FIDIC derived conditions where they are operating within a supply chain governed by a FIDIC main contract.

Employers may also use FIDIC conditions where the local standard conditions of contract are not suited to the procurement route and there is a need to avoid the risks and expense of preparing a bespoke contract.

The different forms of contract within the FIDIC suite are organized around the extent of design and other responsibilities assumed by the Employer and the Contractor. The suite is therefore now aligned with common procurement strategies rather than the nature of the construction works.

Where works are predominantly designed by the Employer, then the Red Book is the appropriate form of contract. Where works are predominantly designed by the Contractor, the Yellow Book is appropriate regardless of whether the works were heavy civil or M&E. The Silver Book is clearly intended for use on Turnkey projects and the Gold Book where the contractor operates the asset in addition to designing and building.

Employers may benefit from utilising FIDIC conditions where potential bidders are from different countries. In such cases the bidders may perceive the use of the familiar FIDIC conditions as increasing the attractiveness of enquiry. This could translate into lower tenders as the contract risks should be better understood by the bidders.

The FIDIC forms can therefore be applied to a wide range of differing engineering and construction projects; from traditional civil engineering to hi-tech windmills and heavy duty oil and gas process plants.

FIDIC has reduced the number of clauses in all of the recent contracts. The Orange Book contained 20 clauses, as now do the Red, Yellow and Silver Books. Previously, the Red Book had 72 clauses.

FIDIC has also standardized the terms across the full suite so that wherever possible the same words and definitions have the same meanings and the clauses are now grouped in a logical manner across all the contracts.

Knowledge of one form of FIDIC conditions is therefore of immediate benefit in respect of other forms.

However, depending on the type of work and the circumstances, the Green Book may be suitable for contracts of considerably greater value.

It is a flexible document containing all the essential administrative and commercial arrangements. It is possible to easily amend and supplement the provisions of the Green Book with differing options incorporated via the Appendix.

The Green Book is likely to be most suited fairly simple or repetitive work or work of short duration without the need for specialist sub-contracts. Under the usual arrangements for this type of contract, the Contractor constructs the Works in accordance with design provided by the Employer. However it may also be suitable for contracts which include, or wholly comprise, the contractor's design.

An area of potential concern for Contractors is that there is no reference to an impartial Engineer in the contract. The contract nominates a member of the Employer's personnel as the authorized person to fulfill the traditional duties of the Engineer.

The intention is that all contract documents will be incorporated in the Appendices to the Agreement. The Appendices will therefore include such documents as the Contractor's offer and the Employer's acceptance together with all the correspondence in between.

The standard General Conditions are intended to be applicable to the majority of projects although it is possible to introduce Particular Conditions if these are required to amend the Green Book and provide for special circumstances of the project.

To assist in the preparation of tender and contract documents Notes for Guidance are included within the Green Book. However these notes do not form part of the Contract.

It is interesting to note that the Green Book includes Rules for Adjudication which is an innovation for a suite of contracts that is traditionally thought of as being relevant to the international market and not domestic to the UK.

Each of the main conditions of contract in the suite now contains a core of common conditions with little significant difference between them.

Amendments to the standard published FIDIC contracts are incorporated by the inclusion of Particular Conditions and guidance on how to prepare the Particular Conditions is published by FIDIC. Where Particular Conditions are incorporated into the contract, care must be taken to ensure that no ambiguity is created, either with the General Conditions or between the clauses in the Particular Conditions. It is essential that all these drafting tasks, and the entire preparation of the contract documents, are entrusted to personnel with the relevant experience of the contractual, technical and procurement aspects of the project.

The suite does not currently include a standard form of subcontract although in 2004 FIDIC stated that a Subcontract form would be a desirable addition to suite. It is expected that if a subcontract form is published that a version for use with the Red Book main contract will be first.

The main forms of contract are described further in some detail below:

Green Book

Short Form of Contract

First Edition 1999

Contents of Contract Book

- Agreement
- General Conditions
- Rules for Adjudication
- Notes for Guidance

The Short Form of Contract is recommended for engineering and building work of relatively small capital value. The Guidance Notes for the Green Book recommended that generally it should not be used on projects with a contract value greater than US$ 500,000.

Red Book

Conditions of Contract for Construction

For Building and Engineering works designed by the Employer

First Edition 1999

Contents of Contract Book

- General Conditions
- Guidance for the Preparation of the Particular Conditions
- Forms of Tender and Contract Agreement
- Dispute Adjudication Agreement

The Red Book provides conditions of contract for construction works where the design is carried out by the Employer. The current Red Book bears little resemblance to its predecessors. Earlier versions of the Red Book were drafted for use on civil engineering projects. The current edition drops the words "civil engineering" from the title and this signifies a move away from the Red Book only being applicable to civil engineering works.

In line with the rest of the FIDIC suite the focus is now more on type of procurement rather than the nature of the works. The Red Book is therefore applicable to any construction works were the Employer carries out the design.

The Red Book is intended for use on projects where the employer carries out the design but it also allows for some elements of the project to be Contractor designed. The Red Book is not suitable for use where most of the works are to be designed by the Contractor and for such projects it would be more appropriate to use the Yellow Book or Silver Book.

As with earlier versions of the Red Book administration of the project and supervision of the works is carried out by an Engineer who is employed by the Employer. The engineer is responsible, amongst other things, for issuing instructions, certifying payments and determining completion.

Payments are normally determined by measurement and applying the rates and prices from the bill of quantities. There is an option for payment to be on the basis of a lump sum.

Where the engineer is required to determine a matter or settle a claim he is required to consult with each of the parties to try and reach an agreement. If agreement cannot be reached the engineer must make a fair determination taking due regard of all relevant circumstances.

If an engineer's determination is not agreed by either of the parties then the dispute will be referred to a Dispute Adjudication Board(DAB) for a decision. The DAB is formed of one or three people who are jointly appointed by the parties. If the decision of the DAB is not accepted by any of the parties then the final step will be resolution via an international arbitration.

The General Conditions and the Particular Conditions together comprise the Conditions of Contract. Guidance is provided in the Red Book for the preparation of Particular Conditions should it be necessary to modify the General Conditions. The Guidance also contains various forms of security such as parent company guarantee, advance payment bond and a retention guarantee which can be selected as applicable to the contract via the Particular Conditions.

This Red Book concludes with example forms for the Letter of Tender, the Appendix to Tender (providing a check-list of the sub-clauses which refer to it), the Contract Agreement, and a Dispute Adjudication Agreement.

Red Book (MDB edition)

Conditions of Contract for Construction

For Building and Engineering works designed by the Employer

MDB Edition 2005

Contents of Contract Book

- General Conditions
- Guidance for the Preparation of the Particular Conditions
- Forms of Tender and Contract Agreement
- Dispute Adjudication Agreement

As part of their standard bidding documents the Multilateral Development Banks (MDBs) have for a number of years required their borrowers or aid recipients to adopt the FIDIC Conditions of Contract.

The FIDIC MDB edition of the Red Book simplifies the use of the FIDIC contract for the MDBs, their borrowers and others involved with project procurement, such as consulting engineers, contractors and contract lawyers.

The following MDBs that have all participated in the preparation of this edition of the Red Book:

- African Development Bank
- Asian Development Bank
- Black Sea Trade and Development Bank

- Caribbean Development Bank
- European Bank for Reconstruction and Development
- Inter-American Development Bank
- International Bank for Reconstruction and Development (The World Bank)
- Islamic Bank for Development Bank
- Nordic Development Fund

It is expected that all of the participating MDBs will adopt this edition of the FIDIC document in their standard bidding documents in the future.

Use of these MDB conditions should significantly reduce the number of additions and amendments to be included in the Particular Conditions.

Nevertheless, most projects will have special requirements which will necessitate some specific changes. The contract therefore retains provision for Particular Conditions as is common with other FIDIC contracts.

As with the main Red Book this MDB edition also includes sample forms for Contract Data, Securities, Bonds, Guarantees and Dispute Board agreements.

In most cases, the amendments which have been made to produce the MDB edition are those arising from the requirements of the MDBs, except for some minor changes of an editorial nature.

However, in the case of the dispute provisions contained in Clauses 20.2 to 20.8 and in the associated Appendix, the opportunity has been taken to make other amendments which FIDIC considered an improvement on the earlier wording as contained in the Red Book 1999 edition.

Yellow Book

Conditions of Contract for

Plant and Design-Build

For electrical and mechanical plant, and for building works, designed by the Contractor

First Edition 1999

Contents of Contract Book

- General Conditions
- Guidance for the Preparation of the Particular Conditions
- Forms of Tender and Contract Agreement
- Dispute Adjudication Agreement

The Yellow Book provides conditions of contract for construction works where the design is carried out by the Contractor. The current Yellow Book bears little resemblance to its predecessors. The current edition drops the words "electrical and mechanical works" from the title and in line with the rest of the FIDIC suite the focus is now more on type of procurement rather than the nature of the works.

The Yellow Book is therefore applicable to the provision of electrical and/or mechanical plant, and for the design and execution of building or engineering works. Under the usual arrangements for this type of contract, the Contractor designs and provides the works in accordance with the Employer's requirements which may include any combination of civil, mechanical, electrical and/or construction works. Administration of the project and supervision of the works is carried out by an Engineer who is employed by the Employer. The Engineer is responsible, amongst other things, for issuing instructions, certifying payments and determining completion. Interim payments of the lump sum Contract Price are made as work proceeds, and are typically based on installments specified in a schedule.

Where the engineer is required to determine a matter or settle a claim he is required to consult with each of the parties to try and reach an agreement. If agreement cannot be reached the engineer must make a fair determination taking due regard of all relevant circumstances. If an engineer's determination is not agreed by either of the parties then the dispute will be referred to a Dispute Adjudication Board for a decision. The DAB is formed by one or three people who are jointly appointed by the parties. If the decision of the DAB is not accepted by any of the parties then the final step will be resolution via an international arbitration.

The General Conditions and the Particular Conditions together comprise the Conditions. Guidance is provided for the preparation of Particular Conditions should it be necessary to modify the General Conditions. The Guidance also contains various forms of security such as parent company guarantee, advance payment bond and a retention guarantee which can be selected as applicable.

The General Conditions as drafted may not suit the Employer's particular needs (for example the standard inclusion of advance payments). Care must be taken in the preparation of the Particular Conditions and completion of the Appendix to avoid creating ambiguities around such conditions. A major area for consideration when preparing Particular Conditions is the risk allocation for ground conditions which is an Employer risk in the standard draft.

The Yellow Book concludes with example forms for the Letter of Tender, the Contract Agreement, and a Dispute Adjudication Agreement.

Orange Book

Conditions of Contract for

Design-Build and Turnkey

First Edition 1995

Contents of Contract Book

- General Conditions
- Guidance for the Preparation of the Particular Conditions
- Forms of Tender and Agreement

The Orange book was published in 1995 to provide a design and build option to the then current FIDIC suite. The Orange Book was the first FIDIC contract to adopt the now current

FIDIC style of drafting and was a template for the drafting teams when preparing the 1999 suite of contracts.

When the Orange book was published the Red and Yellow Books were still aimed at procurement of civil engineering and plant installation respectively. At the time it added a clear design and build and turnkey option into the available suite of contracts.

Since the publication in 1999 of the latest Red and Yellow Books there is now less focus on the type of project and more focus on the implementation of different procurement strategies. It is now likely that an Employer requiring a design and build or turnkey project under a FIDIC contract would use a 1999 edition of the Yellow Book for design and build or a Silver Book for Turnkey.

The Orange Book is drafted for use where the Contractor carries total liability for design. For the Employer, such single-point responsibility may be advantageous, but the benefits may be offset by having less control over the design process and more difficulty in imposing varied requirements.

Under the usual arrangements for a design-build contract, the Contractor is responsible for the design and provision of works. The works may include any combination of engineering (including civil, mechanical, electrical, etc.) and building works.

The Orange Book is intended for use on turnkey contracts, under which the Employer's requirements usually include provision of a fully-equipped facility, ready for operation at the turn of a key. The exact Employer requirements will need to be fully detailed to describe the design, construction, fixtures, fittings and equipment required to be provided by the Contractor's design.

When used for turnkey projects it may be necessary to impose a requirement for the Contractor to operate the Works, either for a few months' commissioning period, or for some years' operation on a build-operate-transfer basis. If this is the case then the FIDIC Gold Book may now be more appropriate.

There are many sub-clauses within the Orange Book which FIDIC decided were generally applicable and these are included in Part I — General Conditions. The Orange Book is arranged to accommodate modification and supplementing of the General Conditions by the inclusion of Part II — Conditions of Particular Application. The Orange Book contains a section of guidance on preparing the Part II conditions. The Part I and Part II conditions together govern the rights and obligations of the parties.

Silver Book

Conditions of Contract for

EPC/Turnkey Projects

First Edition 1999

Contents of Contract Book

- General Conditions
- Guidance for the Preparation of the Particular Conditions

- Forms of Tender and Contract Agreement
- Dispute Adjudication Agreement

The Silver Book is suitable for use on process, power and private-infrastructure projects where a Contractor is to take on full responsibility for the design and execution of a project. Risks for completion to time, cost and quality are transferred to the Contractor and so the Silver Book is only suitable for use with experienced Contractors familiar with sophisticated risk management techniques.

For many large projects construction is only one part of a wider complicated commercial venture and financial or other failure of the construction project will jeopardize the whole venture. The Silver Book approach may suit such projects as it will provide a greater level of cost certainty than can be achieved under the more traditional forms of the FIDIC suite.

To obtain this increased cost certainty the Silver Book requires the Contractor to accept a higher level of risk than is typical under most other forms of contract. The Silver Book transfers the risk of ground conditions to the Contractor. Similarly the Contractor also assumes responsibility, subject to some exceptions, for the accuracy of the Employer's requirements which is a major difference to usual design and build contracts.

Given the high level of risk transfer the Employer must allow time sufficient time in its procurement programme for the Contractor to obtain and consider all relevant information before signing the contract.

Not all risk is passed to the Contractor under the Silver Book and the Employer still retains risks for war, terrorism and Force Majeure. Through the use of Particular Conditions it is possible for the Employer and Contractor to agree alternative risk sharing arrangements before entering into the Contract.

Following award of a project under the Silver Book the Contractor will be given freedom to carry out the work in his chosen manner, provided the end result meets the performance criteria specified by the Employer. Consequently, the Employer should only exercise limited control over the Contractor's work.

There is no reference to an Engineer in the Silver Book. This is because the Employer's reduced influence on the engineering generally. Checking of engineering is more concentrated on validating the end-performance and validating the potential ease of operation, maintenance and spares.

The Silver Book provides conditions relating to "Tests on Completion and Taking Over only takes place after successful completion of the tests. Such provisions are important for EPC/ Turnkey projects where the purpose of the contract is to provide the Employer with a working facility.

Guidance is provided for the preparation of Particular Conditions should it be necessary to modify the General Conditions.

As with the other FIDIC contracts the Silver Book contains various forms of security and concludes with example forms for the Letter of Tender, the Contract Agreement, and a Dispute Adjudication Agreement.

Contract Conditions of Contract for Design, Build and Operate Projects

First Edition 2008

Contents of Contract Book

- General Conditions
- Particular Conditions
- Sample Forms

Following publication of the Orange Book in 1995 and the Red, Yellow and Green Books in 1999 it became clear that there was a growing need for a contract combining a design-build obligation with a long-term operation commitment.

The approach and layout of the DBO contract is more similar to the FIDIC Silver book than any other contract within the FIDIC suite.

The DBO contract adopts a "green-field" DBO scenario with a 20 year operation period and a single contract awarded to a single contracting entity (which will almost certainly be a consortium or joint venture) to optimize the coordination of innovation, quality and performance, rather than award separate contracts for design-build and for operation.

Under the DBO contract the Contractor has no responsibility for either financing the project or for its ultimate commercial success.

The DBO contract, as written, is not suitable for contracts which are not based on the traditional DBO sequence, or where the Operation Period differs significantly from the 20 years adopted.

The document is recommended for general use where tenders are invited on an international basis.

The contract attempts to include all conditions of a general nature, which are likely to apply to the majority of DBO contracts, as General Conditions.

However it is recognized that many employers or governments, or even different jurisdictions, particularly if the conditions were to be used on domestic contracts, may require special conditions of contract, or indeed particular procedures, which differed from those included in the General Conditions.

For this reason, the DBO document Particular Conditions Part B – Special Provisions includes advice to drafters of contract documents who wish to add Special Provisions to replace or supplement the clauses to be found in the General Conditions.

Users who wish to adopt the conditions for use with a different scenario (such as a brown field operate, design, build) or with an operation period significantly different to the 20-year period assumed, are referred to the DBO Contract Guide which identifies the clauses which will require amending by including Special Provisions, and gives comprehensive guidelines and suggestions on how the various issues should be addressed. Successful performance of a long-term DBO contract requires that the parties fully understand the overall time framework and the need for a long-term commitment by both the employer and the contractor. It has therefore been necessary to introduce new procedures and new terminology which are not to be found in the other FIDIC forms of contract.

Contact Details:

fidic@fidic.org

Information for all Member Associations in Africa, Asia Pacific, Europe, the Americas, and the Mid-East is available at: http://www2.fidic.org/regions/

2.4.3 Institution of Civil Engineers (ICE)

ICE is an independent engineering institution and represents approximately 80,000 civil engineers worldwide. Principal membership is in the United Kingdom, but it has memberships in China, Hong Kong, Russia, India and roughly 140 other countries. The ICE documents are traditionally for Engineering Contractors. Pre-1987 versions of FIDIC were very much based on ICE forms but there is far less similarity now. Traditionally they were Engineer based contracts where the Employer appointed the Engineer.

Available Documents

- ICE Conditions of Contract Measurement Version, 7th Edition: July 2004
- ICE Conditions of Contract Design and Construct, 2nd Edition: July 2004
- ICE Conditions of Contract Minor Works, 3rd Edition: July 2004
- ICE Conditions of Contract Term Version: July 2004
- ICE Conditions of Contract Ground Investigation 2nd Edition: July 2004
- Agreement for Consultancy Work in respect of Domestic or Small Works: amendments Dec 1999.

Brief Summary

1. ICE Conditions of Contract, 7th Edition: July 2004

This Contract is based on the traditional pattern of engineer designed contractor built works with valuation by admeasurements. The traditional role of the engineer in advising the client, designing the works, supervising construction, certifying payment and adjudicating in cases of dispute is fully maintained.

2. ICE Conditions of Contract Design and Construct, 2nd Edition: July 2004

This contract radically departs from the normal ICE Conditions of Contract concept with the contractor responsible for all aspects of design and construction, including any design originally provided by or on behalf of the employer. The Form of Tender provides for payment on a lump sum basis but other forms of payment may be used.

3. ICE Conditions of Contract Minor Works, 3rd Edition: July 2004

Intended for use in contracts where:

(*a*) The potential risks involved for both the employer and the contractor are adjudged to be small;

(*b*) The works are of a simple and straight forward nature;

(*c*) The design of the works, save for any design work for which the contractor is made responsible is complete in all essentials before tenders are invited;

(*d*) The contractor has no responsibility for the design of the permanent works other than possibly design of a specialist nature;

(e) Nominated sub-contractors are not employed; and

(f) The contract value does not exceed £500,000 and the period for completion of the contract does not exceed 6 months except where the method of payment is on either a day work or a cost plus fee basis.

4. ICE Conditions of Contract Term Version: July 2004

The concept of a term contract is to carry out routine maintenance and remedial work within a set geographical area. A contractor is appointed to carry out such work for an agreed period of time (the term) carrying out such packages of work as may be required by the employer under conditions set out in the Term Version. The contract should be suitable for planned and reactive maintenance or refurbishment work as well as for new work and emergency works where a contractor may be on call. Each package of work to be carried out is identified in a works order which defines the works required and their location, sets any programming needs and also states any special requirements or payment terms. Payments will normally be valued by measurement using rates set down in the term contract but specially agreed prices or a cost plus arrangement may also be used.

5. ICE Conditions of Contract Ground Investigation, 2nd Edition: July 2004

The conditions are very closely based on the ICE General Conditions of Contract 5th Edition.The contract conditions specify that the work will be under the full direction and control of the engineer, and on site, under the supervision of the engineer's representative or other person appointed by the engineer. The company or firm undertaking the physical work is referred to as the contractor. With limited exceptions, the role of the contractor is to perform the physical works and testing included within the contract documents, the control, direction and interpretation of such work generally being in the hands of the engineer or his representatives. In following the ICE General Conditions of Contract 5th Edition, the contract price is indeterminate at tender stage and is only finally derived on final measurement of the work undertaken.

6. Agreement for Consultancy Work in Respect of Domestic or Small Works: Amendments Dec 1999

ICE has produced this contract for domestic or small works in the form of a checklist for discussion with the client. It is divided into five sections, four of which reflect the type of services most often provided and the fifth deals with payment. These documents can be downloaded from http://www.ice.org.uk/knowledge/downloads_law.asp

2.4.4 The New Engineering Contract (the NEC)

The NEC was developed by ICE in the early 1990s with the aim of introducing a new form of non-adversarial form of contract strategy which would contribute towards the more effective and smoother management of projects.NEC is now in its Third Edition and will be projected as the preferred form of contract for works relating to the 2012 Olympics in London. It is radically different from other English style forms of Building and Civil Engineering Contracts, in that it has a core contract form, written in simple terms and substantial boltons to enable use in a variety of circumstances. The choice of options will have to be a subject for advice in each case.

The NEC is a legal framework of project management procedures designed to handle all aspects of the management of engineering and construction projects. It is in use across the spectrum of engineering and construction activities by a widerange of clients, consultants and contractors. Its use encompasses projects both large and small, civil engineering and building, national and international. It comprises a suite of contract documents and range of support services consisting of training, consultancy, software and a user's group. Since the original launch of the main engineering and construction contract and subcontract, the NEC has been extended to include a professional services contract, an adjudicator's contract and a short contract. Further extensions of, for example, a term services contract, are under development.

The NEC is being used for:

- Engineering and construction work containing any or all of the traditional disciplines such as civil, electrical, mechanical and building work;
- Projects where the Contractor has full design responsibility, partial design responsibility or no design responsibility;
- All the normal current options such as competitive tender, target contracts, cost reimbursable contracts and management contracts; and
- Contracts in the UK and around the world

Structure of the NEC

The main NEC contract, the Engineering and Construction Contract-omnibus edition, and its associated sub-contract, are based on the employer selecting a contract form from six options:

- Option A Priced contract with activity schedule
- Option B Priced contract with bill of quantities
- Option C Target contract with activity schedule
- Option D Target contract with bill of quantities
- Option E Cost reimbursable contract
- Option F Management contract

The chosen contractual approach is then further refined by selecting from up to 15 secondary options depending on the main option selected. These are:

- Option G Performance bond
- Option H Parent company guarantee
- Option J Advance payment to the Contractor
- Option K Multiple currencies
- Option L Sectional completion
- Option M Limitation of the Contractor's liability for his design to reasonable skill and care
- Option N Price adjustment for inflation
- Option P Retention

- Option Q Bonus for early completion
- Option R Delay damages
- Option S Changes in the law
- Option U The Construction (Design and Management) Regulations 1994
- Option V Trust Fund
- Option Z Additional conditions of contract

The Engineering and Construction Short Contract follows the same principles as the main contract but with a reduced number of clauses and no secondary options. It can be used on projects which:

- Do not require sophisticated management techniques;
- Comprise straightforward work; and
- Impose only low risks on both the employer and the contractor.

The Professional Services Contract also follows the broad principles of other NEC documents but has been modified to cover the procurement of professional services.It is designed to be used in one of four main options:

- Option A Priced contract with activity schedule
- Option B Time based contract
- Option C Target contract
- Option D Term contract

These may be supplemented by up to 14 secondary option clauses.

Each contract document is supported by guidance notes and printed flow charts which set out the logic behind all contract decisions. In addition to the contract documents themselves, there are a range of support products and services covering training, consultancy, software, an active users group and a website: http://www.newengineeringcontract.com.

2.4.5 Institution of Electrical Engineers (IEE)

The IEE, based in London, England, is an international organization for electronics, electrical, manufacturing and IT professionals, with specifically tailored products, services and qualifications to meet the needs of today's technology industry. The IEE, jointly with the Institution of Mechanical Engineers (IMechE), issues a range of model forms of general conditions of contract (including, inter alia, Forms of Tender, Agreements and Performance Bonds) and guides (known as "commentaries") to their use. These are Model Forms of Contract for electrical and mechanical work and consultancy. The contents of these publications are decided by a joint committee of IEE/IMechE members and others representing the various interests of the electrical and mechanical engineering industries. IEE has developed the Joint IMechE/IEE Model Forms of General Conditions of Contract. Apart from Model Form MF/4 and Model Form MF/3, the latter not involving the appointment of an engineer to manage the contract, the model forms have also been adopted and are recommended by the Association of Consulting Engineers (ACE).A Model Forms Information

Pack which expands on the Model Forms and which contains copies of all Supplements, Amendment Slips and Amendment Lists relating to the current range of Model Forms is available on the IEE website.

Contact Website: http://www.iee.org/Publish/Books/Model/index.cfm

2.4.6 Institute of Chemical Engineers

IChemE is a similar organization to IMechE/IEE, but specializes in production of contracts for the specialist process industry. The form of contract has been significantly updated in recent years to cover the spectrum of contract possibilities. Like FIDIC, IChemE contracts are often known by their colour and a list of available contracts is set out below:

- IChemE (Green) Form of Contract – Reimbursable Contracts
- IChemE (Brown) Form of Contract – Subcontract for Civil Engineering Works
- IChemE (Grey) Form of Contract – Adjudication Procedures
- IChemE (Orange) Minor Works 2nd ed 2003
- IChemE (Pink) Form of Contract – Arbitration Procedures
- IChemE (Red) Form of Contract – Lump Sum Contracts
- IChemE (White) Rules for Expert Determination 3rd ed 2001
- IChemE (Yellow) Sub Contracts 3rd ed 2003
- IChemE (Green) Reimbursable

2.4.7 The Joint Contracts Tribunal (JCT)

The Joint Contracts Tribunal (JCT), which represents a cross-section of the construction industry including employers and construction clients, contractors, consultants and specialists, was established in 1931 and has for many decades produced (and still produces) standard forms of contracts, guidance notes and other standard documentation for use in the construction industry.

It consists of members of the professional association of architects, consulting engineers, the construction confederation, specialist contractors council and the institute of chartered surveyors. The standard form building contract JCT 2005 is regarded as the industry standard for "general" or traditional style contracting. It is based on a common origin with the Irish RIAI form of contract and embodies broadly similar principles. However, it is much more detailed. There are six versions of the JCT contract, with quantities, with approximate quantities and without quantities with a private and Local Authority edition (equivalent to the Irish GLDA) in each case. Certain further supplements are available. These include a contractor designed portion supplement (CDPS).

There are sub-contracting forms for use with the JCT 2005. These include a standard form of sub-contract tender and agreement, a standard form of agreement between the sub-contractor and nominated contractor, employer nominated sub-contractor agreement. The intermediate form of building contract IFC 98 is shorter than JCT 2005 but is still fairly complex. It is designed for work that uses basic trade skills of the industry and does not require complex building services, engineering packages. CD 98 is the standard design and build form of contract. There is no architect administering the contract. It is set on the basis of the document called the employer's requirements which specifies what the contractor is being asked to do.

The 2005 JCT Contracts

The JCT has revised the standard form of construction contracts in the "2005 series". The following forms of contract have been modified and updated from earlier versions of these contracts;

- Standard Building Contract with Quantities (SBC/Q)
- Standard Building Contract with Approximate Quantities (SBC/AQ)
- Standard Building Contract without quantities (SBC/XQ)
- Design Build Contract (DB)
- Intermediate Building Contract (IC)
- Intermediate Building Contract with contracts design (ICD)
- Minor Works Building Contract (MW)
- Minor Works Building Contract with Contract to Design (MBW)

There are a number of companion guides to the forms have been published and are available on line. Each of the 2005 JCT Contracts adopt a similar structure and are divided into Articles of Agreement, conditions and various schedules. The conditions are divided into the following broad parts:

- Carrying out of works
- Control of the works
- Payments
- Variation
- Injury damage and insurance
- Assignment third party rights and collateral warranties
- Termination
- Settlement of disputes

The JCT 2005 contracts provide for the following direct warranties:

- Contractor to funder
- Contractor to purchaser/tenant
- Sub-Contractor to employer
- Sub-Contractor to funder
- Sub-Contractor to purchaser/tenant

The employer is to stipulate which third party rights or warranties are required.

Collateral Warranties

The 2005 series of JCT Contracts use the Third Party Rights Act 1999. This Act allows parties to a contract to confer benefits and rights directly on a third party who is not a party to the contract. Effect is given by service by the employer of a notice to the effect that the named purchaser or tenant has a specified interest in the works. The Collateral Warranties are in broadly similar terms to those found in Ireland. For example under the Collateral Warranty with a purchaser/tenant, the contractor warrants with the purchaser and tenant that the works have been undertaken in accordance with the main contract. The contractor is liable for the reasonable cost and repair and reinstatement of works. The collateral warranty allows for the possibility of the contractor being liable for additional losses incurred by the purchaser/tenant up to a maximum figure.

The default position under the contractor's collateral warranty is that the contractor is liable only for repair and reinstatement costs and not additional liability unless specified. The contractor's liability is limited to a just and equitable share of losses on the basis that any consultants specified in the contract particulars have paid a share of the loss concerned. The contractor is entitled to raise any term of the contract or other rights in defence of liability as would be available against the employer.

The purchaser and tenant's rights are assignable twice. They may be assigned by absolute assignment to any person taking a transfer of the original purchaser or tenant's interests. The rights for funders/banks are in broadly similar terms. Provision is made for "step-in" rights on behalf of the lending institution/funds. The contractor is not to terminate the employment without copying the funder with notice. Certain other notices must be copied to the funder. The lending institution has seven days in which to intervene and take over the contract under the step-in provisions.

JCT 2005 Sub-Contract

There are two sets of JCT Sub-Contract documents for use with the above mentioned main contract. One is for use where there is a sub-contractor design portion and the other is for use where the sub-contractor has no design responsibilities. For each, there is a form of agreement and set of conditions:

- Standard Building and Sub-Contract Agreement (SBC Sub/A)
- Standard Building and Sub-Contract Conditions (SBC Sub/C)
- Standard Building and Sub-Contract with Sub-Contractor's Design Agreement (SPC Sub/D/A)
- Standard Building and Sub-Contract with Sub-Contractor Design Conditions (SBC Sub/D/C)

There is a guide to the forms known as SPC Sub/G. There are further forms of sub-contract for use with Design and Build Contracts. These are the Design and Build Sub-Contract Agreement (DBSUB/A) and a Design and Build Sub-Contract Conditions (DBSUB/C). The Companion guide is DBSUB/G).

Contact: http://www.jctcontracts.com

2.4.8 The Association of Consultant Architects (ACA)

ACA is the national professional body representing architects in private practices throughout the UK. ACA has drawn up its own form of Building Contract with ancillary documents. In 2000 it published the first construction industry Project Partnership Contract PPC2000.

Available Documents

- PPC2000 - ACA Standard Form of Contract for Project Partnering (Amended 2003)
- SPC2000 - ACA Standard Form of Specialist Contract for Project Partnering (Amended 2004)

- ACA Form of Building Agreement 1982 Third Edition 1998 (2003 Revision)
- ACA98 The Appointment of a Consultant Architect For Small Works
- Content and Specialist Services (2000 Edition)

Brief Summary

1. PPC2000

PPC2000 is a multi-party non-adversarial construction contract that provides the foundation for the partnering process. It allows the client, the constructor and all consultants and key specialists to sign a single Partnering Contract. It also provides for the early selection of a project partnering team and the collaborative finalization of designs, prices and members of the supply chain. It covers the full duration of the partnering relationships and provides for a partnering timetable to govern the contributions of all partnering team members to partnered activities. PPC2000 also provides for a clear system of reducing, managing and sharing risks and offers a non-adversarial problem resolution mechanism.

2. SPC2000

SPC2000 is a specialist contract for project partnering and is a specialist subcontractor version of PPC2000, following a similar format. SPC2000 complements PPC2000 and focuses on the involvement of specialist sub-contractors in project design and risk management from the earliest stage of a project and encourages collaborative work throughout all stages of project process.

3. ACA Form of Building Agreement 1982, Third Edition 1998 (2003 Revision)

This contract ensures that responsibilities are placed fairly upon those parties best able to shoulder them. It defines the various responsibilities of the parties in a readable and easily understood way, eliminating areas of uncertainty. The flexibility of this contract is achieved via the use of key optional clauses providing for a number of choices which allow it to be tailored to the needs of each individual building project. It can be used for design, development and construction.

4. ACA98 the Appointment of a Consultant Architect for Small Works, Works of Simple Content and Specialist Services (2000 Edition)

This contract can be used between the architect and the client for small building projects and also for projects where the content of the work is of a simple nature.

Contact: Website: http://www.acarchitects.co.uk

2.4.9 BE Collaborative Contract

The BE Collaborative Contract is a new form of contract for construction projects that underpins collaborative behavior. The contract has been created by BE (Collaborating for the Built Environment). BE is the largest independent association for companies across the supply chain in the UK, committed to the research, design and delivery of sustainable built development. The Collaborative Contract is a new contract framework for the delivery of successful construction projects. This contract is intended for use by parties who genuinely want a contractual framework that assists a collaborative approach and who want to identify and manage risks, rather than simply passing them on under contract conditions. The BE Collaborative Contract aims to underpin collaborative behaviour, provide flexibility in use and be clear and concise. The BE Collaborative Contract is available for purchase in various formats from two online retailers.

Contract: Website: http://www.beonline.co.uk

2.4.10 GC Form of Contract

GC forms of contract originated from the CCC/Works family which was extensively used for Government Contracts until the 1970s. The CCC form became increasingly antiquated and fell into disuse. In 1998 the forms were revamped and reissued as the GC set of forms and have been used for non government contracts since that time. The set covers almost every permutation and is an alternative to use of the JCT or NEC form.

A summary of the forms available is:

- GC Works 1 – 1998 Without Quantities
- GC Works 1 – 1998 With Quantities
- GC Works 1 – 1998 Single State Design and Build
- GC Works 1 – 1998 Model Forms and Commentary
- GC Works 1 – 1998 Two Stage Design and Build
- GC Works 1 – Construction Management Trade Contract 1999 with quantities
- GC Works 1 – Construction Management Trade Contract 1999 without quantities
- GC Works 2 – 1998 Minor Works – General Conditions and Supporting Model Documents
- GC Works 3 – 1998 Contract for M&E Engineering Works – General Conditions and Supporting Model Documents
- GC Works 4 – 1998 Contract for Building, CE, M&E Small Works
- GC Works 5 – Commentary 2000
- GC/Works 5 – 1999 General Condition for the Appointment of Consultants: framework agreement
- GC Works 6 – 1999 Day works Term Contract
- GC Works 7 – Measured Term Contract
- GC Works 8 – Specialist Term Contract
- GC Works 9 – 1999 Lump Sum Term Contract for operation, maintenance and repair of M&E Plant Equipment and Installations
- GC Works 10 – 2000 – Facilities Management
- GC Works 11 – 2000 Minor Works Term Contract – general conditions, model forms and commentary
- GC Works – Sub-Contract General Conditions
- GC Works – Sub-Contract Model Forms
- GC Works – Sub-Contract Guidance Note

2.4.11 International Chamber of Commerce (ICC)

The Commission on Commercial Law and Practice (CLP) (one of the Commissions of the ICC), based in Paris, France, is in the process of developing ICC model contracts and ICC model clauses, which give parties a neutral framework for their contractual relationships. These contracts and clauses are carefully drafted by the experts of the CLP Commission without expressing a bias for anyone particular legal system. The idea behind ICC model contracts and clauses is to provide a sound legal basis upon which parties to international contracts can quickly establish an even-handed agreement acceptable to both sides. The contracts are constructed to protect the interests of all parties, combining a single framework of rules with flexible provisions allowing the parties to insert their own requirements. Currently, the following ICC model contracts are being developed:

- ICC Model Turnkey Supply of an Industrial Plant Contract
- ICC Model Major Project Turnkey Contract

Contact: Website: http://www.iccwbo.org/law/contracts/

2.4.12 ORGALIME

Liaison Group of the European Mechanical, Electrical, Electronic and Metalworking Industries (ORGALIME). ORGALIME issued a new standard contract – the ORGALIME Turnkey Contract for Industrial Works – its most comprehensive contract publication to date. ORGALIME's premise was that purchasers and contractors in the engineering sector, who had used existing models, had not found them as suitable for industrial works as for civil engineering contracts. Orgalime publication aim to provide the European engineering industries with documents that can help industry to draw up adequate business contracts and give practical advice on frequently occurring legal questions. The publication are, for the most part, drafted by Orgalime Member Association Lawyer.

Chapter 3 THE LEGAL FRAMEWORK

3.1 INTRODUCTION

The description which follows is a general description intended to give a basic familiarity with the Court System. There are many exceptions to the general principles stated. There are two principal systems of law that operate in the world. These are:

(*i*) Common Law

(*ii*) Civil Law

Common Law is the system used in the UK, the USA, Canada, Australia, India and most of the countries that were part of the British Empire. The Civil Law system is found in most of mainland Europe and in countries around the world associated with them.

It is important to realize that the term 'Civil Law' is also used to denote both the 'System' and non criminal matters in Common Law Countries.

The Courts in England and Wales exist in what is termed a 'common law' jurisdiction. It shares this distinction with other English speaking countries, such as Ireland, USA, Canada, Australia, New Zealand and some non-English speaking countries, such as India. The system owes its origins to the legal system of England. Common-law legal systems place greater emphasis on previous court decisions than do 'civil-law jurisdictions, such as France and other European countries. Those legal systems trace their origins back to Roman Law and, more recently, the legal codifications instituted by Napoleon Bonaparte.

Lawyers operating in common-law jurisdictions therefore need to work more closely with case-law than do lawyers operating in civil-law countries because the English Courts are bound by their previous decisions. This is known as the principle of stare-decisis.(let the decision stand).

3.2 CLASSIFICATIONS OF LAW

Law as distinct from the Systems may generally be divided into two broad categories:

Civil: This center on the person wronged, aiming to compensate him or to prevent further wrongs being committed against him. Duties towards the person wronged may arise either out of contract or from a relationship imposed by law.

Criminal: This centers on the wrongdoer, aiming to punish offenders and to deter others from committing crimes. Where a criminal statute empowers the court to order compensation, this is very much a secondary aim of the sentencing process. Duties towards the person wronged arise entirely out of a relationship imposed by law.

3.3 THE DOCTRINE OF PRECEDENT

The Common Law develops through its case law. This development is dependent upon the cases which are brought before the courts day by day. In formulating their judgments, the judges review the existing body of cases and apply them to similar situations. Many of the principles which are applied are derived from ancient customary law and from Roman law. It is often said that judges do not make law but merely declare the existing law. This concept requires an efficient system of law reporting so that the existing law is accessible to litigants who need to be able to predict their likely chances of success.

The court rarely has to decide on cases which are based on identical facts. If a similar case has been decided, this is likely to be conclusive in subsequent cases. But no two cases are exactly alike—the law applied in previous cases must be extended to meet new situations and so the law moves on. Some judges are very ready to extend the existing principle of law to meet the developing social values of society; others are more cautious. Judges are aware that, in order to be fair to all, the law must be certain and the outcome of any case must be reasonably predictable. If judges were not bound by the previously decided cases, no one could predict the likely outcome of a case and the risks of litigation would be unacceptable. If the law has a degree of certainty, the parties will be more likely to negotiate a fair settlement of their differences out of court. Judges must also be very careful to avoid making new law. Under the doctrine of separation of powers, this is the function of Parliament.

3.4 PROCEDURE RULES

The Procedure Rules govern court proceedings and careful attention has to be paid to them. Procedure Rules differ in jurisdictions so care must be taken to comply with those of the local jurisdiction. CPR does give a clear idea of 'best practice' but this does not supplant the local rules.

Chapter 4 COURT SYSTEM

4.1 INDIA

4.1.1 Introduction

The Judiciary of India is an independent body and is separate from the Executive and Legislative bodies of the Indian Government. The judicial system of India is stratified into various levels. At the apex is the Supreme Court, which is followed by High Courts at the state level, District Courts at the district level.

INDIAN LEGAL HIERARCHY

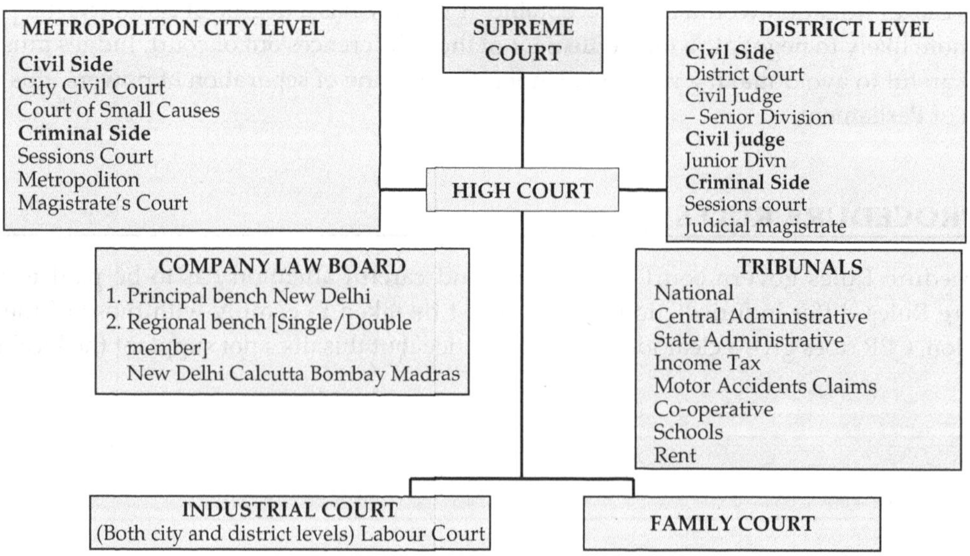

4.1.2 Supreme Court

The Supreme Court is the highest judicial body in India. The Supreme Court came into power on 28th January 1950; just two days after the Constitution of India came to effect. In the initial stages, it had its office in a part of the Parliament House. The Supreme Court is endowed with many duties and responsibilities. The biggest responsibility is that it is the highest court of appeal and is also the protector of the Constitution in the country.

The Chief Justice of India and 25 other judges make up the Supreme Court of India. The appointments are done directly by the President of India. There are certain criteria that have to be fulfilled by the advocates to become a judge of the Supreme Court. Being a citizen of India is one of the most important criteria. Apart from this, the person has to have an experience of minimum five years as a judge in the High Court or any other two courts one after another. He should also be a prominent jurist as per the President of the country, so that he can take up responsibilities well. The Chief Justice is also consulted at the time of appointment of the judges in the Supreme Court.

The Judges of the Supreme Court are free to exercise their power as and when required. The process of removal of the Supreme Court judges is quite an interesting but lengthy process. An order from the President is mandatory in case of removal of the judges. A two-thirds majority has to be obtained from both the houses for the removal of the judges.

The jurisdiction of the Supreme Court is divided into original jurisdiction, advisory jurisdiction and appellate jurisdiction. Original jurisdiction is required when there is a dispute between the Government and the states of India or anyone state of India. The Supreme Court can also enforce fundamental Rights according to the Article 32 of the Constitution of India.

The appellate jurisdiction is mentioned in Articles 132(1), 133(1) or 134 of the Constitution. The decision of the High Court can be questioned in the Supreme Court of the country. One can appeal to the Supreme Court, if he or she is not satisfied with the decision of the High Court. The Supreme Court has the provision of accepting or rejecting the case at its own discretion. There are also provisions of pardoning criminals and canceling their lifetime imprisonment or death sentence by the Supreme Court.

Apart from the original and appellate jurisdiction of the Supreme Court, there is an advisory jurisdiction that needs special mention. There are many cases that are directly referred by the President of India and the Supreme Court has to look into those matters. This provision is mentioned in Article 143 of the Indian Constitution.

The Supreme Court in India acts as an independent body and is free from any outer control. The contempt of law court in India is a punishable offence and the Supreme Court takes care of this immaculately.

4.1.3 High Courts

There are High Courts in almost all the states of India and the Union Territories. The High Courts work under the Supreme Court in the country. These courts are vested with lot of power. They decide on both civil as well as criminal cases. Most of the cases that are handled by the High Courts of the country are passed on from the district or lower courts.

The judges of the High Courts are appointed by the President of India, in consultation with the Chief justice of India and the Governor of the state. The Chief Justice heads each of the High

Courts in India. The numbers of judges vary from one court to other depending on the area that the High Court covers and the number of cases that it handles. There are also High Courts that serve more than one Indian state or Union Territory. Each of these courts have original and appellate jurisdiction under them. Summons can also be issued by the High Court. Revenue matters are dealt by original jurisdiction, while an eminent jury handles original criminal cases.

Established in the year 1862, the Calcutta High Court is the oldest court in India. Apart from this, there are 18 total High Courts in the country, some of which are Bombay High Court, Delhi High Court, Chhattisgarh High Court, Gujarat High Court, Jharkhand High Court, Madras High Court, Patna High Court and Sikkim High Court.

4.1.4 District Courts

District courts established by the State governments in India for every district or for one or more districts together taking into account the number of cases, population distribution in the district. They administer justice in India at a district level. These courts are under administrative control of the High Court of the State to which the district concerned belongs. The decisions of District court is subject to the appellate jurisdiction of the High court.

The highest court in each district is that of the District and Sessions Judge. This is the principal court of original civil jurisdiction besides High Court of the State and which derives its jurisdiction in civil matters primarily from the code of civil procedure. The district court is also a court of Sessions when it exercises its jurisdiction on criminal matters under Code of Criminal procedure. The district court is presided over by one District Judge appointed by the state Government. In addition to the district judge there may be number of Additional District Judges and Assistant District Judges depending on the workload. The Additional District Judge and the court presided have equivalent jurisdiction as the District Judge and his district court.

However, the district judge has supervisory control over Additional and Assistant District Judges, including decisions on allocation of work among them. The District and Sessions judge is often referred to as "district judge" when he presides over civil matters and "sessions judge" when he presides over criminal matters. Being the highest judge at district level, the District Judge also enjoys the power to manage the state funds allocated for the development of judiciary in the district.

The district judge is also called "Metropolitan session judge" when he is presiding over a district court in a city which is designated "Metropolitan area" by the state Government. Other courts subordinated to district court in the Metropolitan area are also referred to with "metropolitan" prefixed to the usual designation. An area is designated a metropolitan area by the concerned state Government if population of the area exceeds one million.

Appointment of district judge and other Additional and Assistant district judges is done by the state Government in consultation with the High court of the state. A minimum of seven years of practice as a lawyer at bar is a necessary qualification. Upon a written examination and oral interview by a committee of High court judges, the appointment of district judges is notified by the state Government. This is referred to as direct recruitment. District judges are also appointed by way of elevation of judges from courts subordinate to district courts provided they fulfill the minimum years of service.

A district judge or Additional judge may be removed from his office by the state Government in consultation with the High court. The next level of ascendancy for a district judge who served sufficient number of years is the post of High court judge. High court Judges are usually appointed from a pool of advocates practicing at the Bar of the High court and District Judges who served for sufficient number of years. By virtue of his office a district judge often occupies privileged position in the district alongside administrative heads of the district like the collector.

The District Court or Additional District court exercises jurisdiction both on original and appellate side in civil and criminal matters arising in the District. The territorial and pecuniary jurisdiction in civil matters is usually set in concerned state enactments on the subject of civil courts. On the criminal side jurisdiction is almost exclusively derived from code of criminal procedure. This code sets the maximum sentence which a district court may award which currently is capital punishment.

The court exercises appellate jurisdiction over all subordinate courts in the district on both civil and criminal matters. These subordinate courts usually consist of a Junior Civil Judge court, Principal Junior civil Judge court, Senior civil judge court (often called sub court)in the order of ascendancy on the civil side and the Judicial Magistrate Court of IInd Class, Judicial Magistrate Court of Ist class, Chief Judicial Magistrate Court in the order of ascendancy on the criminal side.

Certain matters on criminal or civil side cannot be tried by a court inferior in jurisdiction to a district court if the particular enactment makes a provision to the effect. This gives the District Court original jurisdiction in such matters.

Appeals from the district courts lie to the High court of the concerned state.

4.2 AMERICA

4.2.1 Introduction

Most states organize courts into three basic levels, although the states vary in their names for these courts. The system follows a basic structure of Trial Court, Appellate Court and Supreme Court, with the Supreme Court as the highest court of law for the state. These three levels remain the same for both civil and criminal cases.

CIVIL COURT STRUCTURE

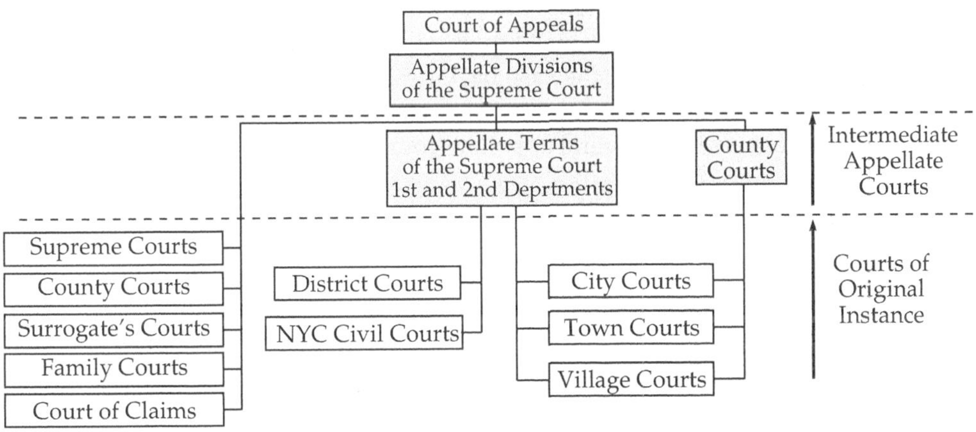

CRIMINAL COURT STRUCTURE

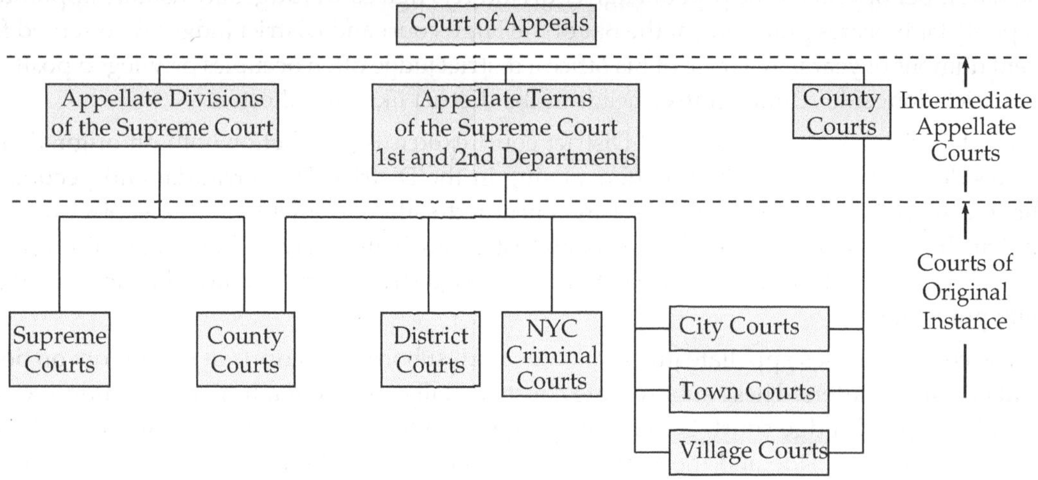

4.2.2 Trial Courts

Trial courts are usually the first type of court people use when they file a lawsuit or face a criminal charge. Courts at this level may try cases before a jury or judge who serves as fact-finders, or deciders, if the case goes to trial. Most cases never go to trial, however; they are settled, decided, dismissed or pleaded out at a pre-trial stage, with or without a court decision. Many states use different types of trial courts—such as family law courts, domestic violence courts or traffic courts—that handle only cases within their area of law. Additionally, small-claims courts often handle cases concerning smaller amounts of money.

4.2.3 Appellate Courts

Apellate courts do not do trials. Instead, they hear certain types of issues that a party to the trial court case claims the trial court has decided in error. Appellants claim errors by arguing that the trial court has used the wrong law or dismissed a case wrongly, for example. In criminal cases, appellants can claim that the trial court has decided sentences or trials wrongly, that new evidence has been discovered, or the trial court defense lawyer was ineffective. Sometimes a party to a case may appeal issues during the trial; most make their appeal after the trial. If the appellate court agrees with the appellant, it may send the case back for a new trial, or reverse part of the trial court's verdict or decision. Occasionally, a party may go directly to the appellate level for some extreme exigency. A state may have several appellate courts.

4.2.4 Supreme Court

One court acts as the highest court for each state. It too serves an appellate court, so it reviews relevant trial and appellate court decisions in order to reach a final decision. Usually, supreme courts only hear issues important to the public, or decide between conflicting lines of law coming from different appellate courts about the same basic issue. All courts in the state have to follow the supreme court's decision on a specific issue.

4.3 ENGLISH AND WALES

4.3.1 Introduction

The court system has a hierarchical structure. The courts at the bottom of the hierarchy — the Magistrates Courts and the County Court — serve their own area and deal with the vast majority of cases in England and Wales. They are known as Inferior Courts, as their jurisdiction is limited by geography or by the monetary value at stake in the case. Their decisions are not recorded and are not binding on other courts. More important cases are heard in the Superior Courts — the High Court for civil matters and the Crown Court for criminal matters. The Court of Appeal and the Supreme Court, as appeal courts, are also superior courts. All superior courts are Courts of Record. This means that an official record is kept of their proceedings and the decisions of the court are binding on other courts at the same level or below them in the hierarchy.

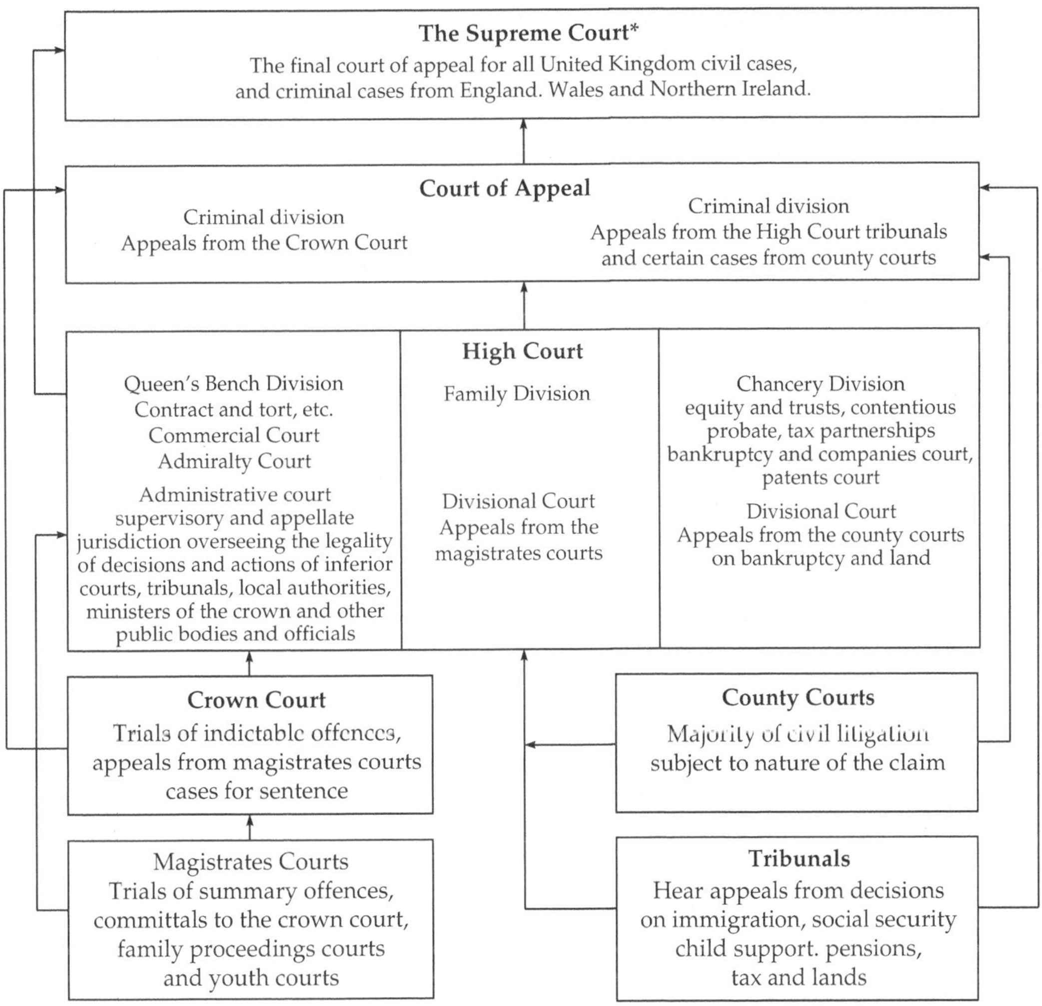

(* not administered by HMCS)

4.3.2 The Civil Court System

4.3.2.1 The Magistrates' Court

(*i*) The Magistrates' Court has a civil jurisdiction in family matters under which they make custody orders relating to children and maintenance orders in matrimonial and domestic cases. They also deal with adoption proceedings. They can make orders excluding a family member from the household.

(*ii*) Appeals on family matters are heard by the Family Division of the High Court.

4.3.2.2 The County Court

This is the lowest tier of the civil court system. The county courts have jurisdiction over recovery of debts and civil actions. In recent years, the High Court has become over loaded and therefore subject to very long delays. The financial limit on the County Court's jurisdiction has therefore been raised substantially in order for more cases to be dealt with at this level which is more cost effective both to the parties to litigation and to the public exchequer. The Lord Chancellor now has power to allocate work between the High Court and the County Court. Appeals from the County Court on bankruptcy petitions are dealt with by the Chancery Division of the High Court. Appeals on other matters are heard by the Court of Appeal.

4.3.2.3 The High Court

Until recently, the High Court sat in the Royal Courts of Justice in the Strand and High Court judges travelled out from there to local courts. Now-a-days, much High Court business is dealt with in High Court District Registries situated in buildings of the larger County Courts. The High Court is both an original court and an appellate court. It is possible to begin court proceedings in the High Court and it also hears appeals from lower courts. Rules of Procedure in the High Court are found in "The Rules of Supreme Court"— also known as the White Book. The High Court is divided into three divisions:

(*a*) The Queen's Bench Division

(*b*) The Chancery Division

(*c*) The Family Division.

The three courts have separate jurisdictions. No limit is set on the jurisdiction of the High Court. It serves the whole of England and Wales.

4.3.2.4 The Queen's Bench Division

The President of the Queen's Bench Division is the Lord Chief Justice. In addition to its criminal jurisdiction, the QBD hears tort and contract cases. The QBD also has judges who specialize in hearing commercial cases and admiralty cases in the Commercial Court and the Admiralty Court which have different procedures from the other QBD courts.

In civil matters, the QBD hears appeals for District Judges in the County Courts and from some tribunals.

4.3.2.5 The Chancery Division

(*i*) The President of the Division is the Lord Chancellor but in practice he never sits. The effective head of the court is the Vice Chancellor.

(*ii*) Most chancery actions are heard in London. The Chancery Division tries matters concerned with trusts, company matters, insolvency, cases relating to land and patent and trademark actions which are heard in a special court. The Court of Protection, which oversees the property and affairs of mental patients, is also part of the Chancery Division.

4.3.2.6 The Family Division

(*i*) The head of the court is the President of the Family Division. The court hears all defended matrimonial cases, which are rare now-a-days. The Family Division makes declarations of legitimacy and of the validity or invalidity of marriages. It hears proceedings for the presumption of death, ward ship, adoption, guardianship and some matrimonial property matters.

(*ii*) The Family Division hears appeals on matrimonial and family matters from the County Court and the Magistrates' Court.

4.3.2.7 The Court of Appeal

(*i*) In both criminal and civil matters, the Court of Appeal has its own judges known as the Lords Justices of Appeal. Cases are also heard by ex officio judges (judges who sit by reason of the office they hold): the Lord Chancellor, the Master of the Rolls, the President of the Family Division, the Lord Chief Justice, the Vice Chancellor, the judges from the Supreme Court and former Lord Chancellors.

(*ii*) Usually three judges sit together but where they are hearing a very difficult or significant point of law, five judges will hear the case.

(*iii*) The Civil Division of the Court of Appeal hears appeals from lower civil courts.

4.3.2.8 The Supreme Court

(*i*) The Supreme Court hears appeals from:

(*a*) The Court of Appeal (when leave to appeal is granted either by the Court of Appeal or on application for leave to the Supreme Court);

(*b*) The High Court (with the permission of the Supreme Court) — where there is a point of law of general public importance, the case can leapfrog from the High Court direct to the Supreme Court.

4.3.3 The Criminal Court System

4.3.3.1 Magistrates and Youth Court

(*i*) Magistrates Courts are presided over by a bench of lay magistrates (or justices of the peace), or a legally-trained district judge (formerly known as a stipendiary magistrate), sitting in each local justice area. There are no juries.

(*ii*) They hear minor criminal cases, as well as certain licensing applications. Youth courts are run on similar lines to Adult magistrates' courts but deal with offenders aged between the ages of 10 and 17 inclusive. Youth courts are presided over by a specially trained subset of experienced Adult Magistrates or a District Judge. Youth Magistrates have a wider catalogue of disposals available to them for dealing with young offenders and often hear more serious cases against youths (which for adults would normally be dealt with by the Crown Court). Youth courts are not open to the public for observation, only the parties involved in a case being admitted.

4.3.3.2 Crown Courts

(*i*) The Crown Court is a criminal court of both original and appellate jurisdiction which in addition handles a limited amount of civil business both at first instance and on appeal. It was established by the Courts Act of 1971. It replaced the Assizes whereby High Court judges would periodically travel around the country hearing cases, and Quarter Sessions which were periodic county courts. The Old Bailey is the unofficial name of London's most famous Criminal Court, which is now part of the Crown Court. Its official name is the "Central Criminal Court". The Crown Court also hears appeals from Magistrates' Courts.

(*ii*) The Crown Court is only a superior court in connection with its jurisdiction to hear trials on indictment. In other cases, such as when hearing an appeal from a Magistrates' Court or exercising civil jurisdiction, it is an inferior court and may be subject to judicial review.

4.3.3.3 Appeals

(*i*) The Court of Appeal

(*ii*) The Supreme Court

4.4 HONG KONG

4.4.1 Introduction

The courts of justice in Hong Kong are the Court of Final Appeal, the High Court (which comprises the Court of Appeal and the Court of First Instance), the District Court, the Magistrates' Courts, the Coroner's Court, and the Juvenile Court. In addition, there are a number of tribunals which have jurisdiction to adjudicate on disputes relating to specific, defined areas. These include the Lands Tribunal, the Labour Tribunal, the Small Claims Tribunal and the Obscene Articles Tribunal.

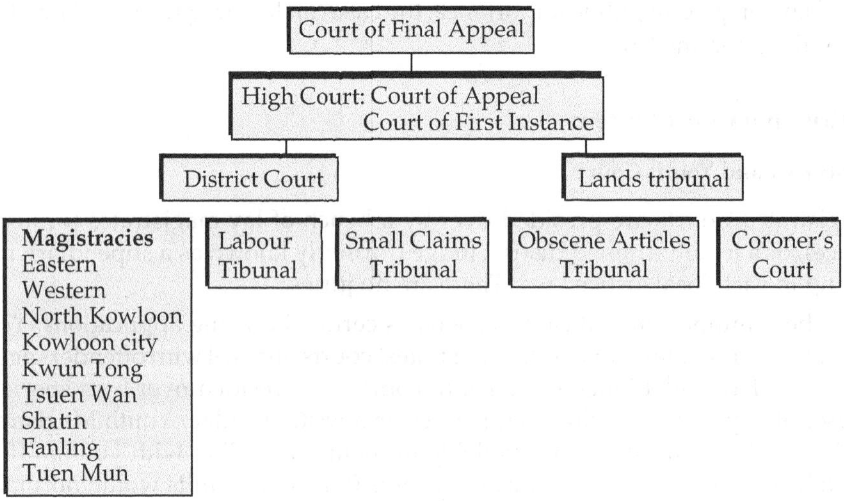

4.4.2 The Court of Final Appeal

Established on 1 July 1997 upon the commencement of the Hong Kong Court of Final Appeal Ordinance. It is the highest appellate court in Hong Kong and hears appeals on civil and criminal matters from the High Court. The Court, when sitting, will comprise five judges — the Chief Justice, three permanent judges and one non-permanent Hong Kong judges or one judge from other common law jurisdictions. At present, there are eleven judges on the list of non-permanent Hong Kong judges and four judges on the list of judges from other common law jurisdictions.

4.4.3 The High Court

Headed by the Chief Judge, the High Court consists of the Court of Appeal and the Court of First Instance.

4.4.3.1 The Court of Appeal of the High Court

Hears appeals on civil and criminal matters from the Court of First Instance and the District Court, as well as appeals from the Lands Tribunal. It also makes rulings on questions of law referred to it by the lower courts. There are nine Justices of Appeal at present.

4.4.3.2 The Court of First Instance of the High Court

Has unlimited jurisdiction in both civil and criminal matters. It also exercises jurisdiction in bankruptcy, company winding-up, adoption, probate and mental health matters. The most serious criminal offences, such as murder, manslaughter, rape, armed robbery, complex commercial frauds and drug offences involving large quantities, are tried by a judge of the Court of First Instance, sitting with a jury consisting of seven or, when a judge so orders, nine. It is the jury which decides whether the accused is guilty or not guilty. There are twenty-five Judges of the Court of First Instance at present.

4.4.3.3 The Lands Tribunal

Have four principal judicial functions. Firstly, it determines the sums payable by the government and others for compensation to persons whose land is compulsorily resumed or its value reduced because of public or private developments. Secondly, the tribunal has an appellate jurisdiction from the decisions by the Commissioner of Rating and Valuation and the Director of Housing. Thirdly, the Tribunal may, under the Landlord and Tenant (Consolidation) Ordinance which categorizes premises into four parts, make orders for possession and consequential relief, grant a new tenancy and determine prevailing market rent. Fourthly, the Tribunal hears and determines building management matters and disputes specified under the Building Management Ordinance.

There is a President of the Tribunal who is a Court of First Instance Judge. At present, there are two Presiding Officers who are District Judges as well as two Members who are surveyors.

4.4.3.4 The District Court

Has civil jurisdiction to hear monetary claims over $50,000 and upto $1,000,000 or, where the claims are for recovery of land, the annual rent or rate able value does not exceed $240,000. In its criminal jurisdiction, the court may try more serious cases, with the exception of murder, manslaughter and rape. The maximum term of imprisonment it may impose is seven years. The Family Court, which is part of the District Court, deals with family-related matters such as divorce and adoption.

There is a Chief District Judge and thirty-three District Judges. Four District Judges sit in the Family Court.

4.4.3.5 The Magistracy

Magistrates exercise criminal jurisdiction over a widerange of offences. Although there is a general limit of two years imprisonment or a fine of $100,000, many ordinances give magistrates the power to sentence up to three years imprisonment and to impose larger fines, in some cases up to $5,000,000. All indictable offences originate in a Magistracy but the Secretary for Justice may apply to have a case transferred to the District Court or committed to the Court of First Instance of the High Court depending on the seriousness of the case. Appeals from the Magistrate's Court are heard by a Judge of the Court of First Instance of the High Court. There are a Chief Magistrate, ten Principal Magistrates and fifty-one Magistrates at present. Cases of a more routine and minor nature, such as hawking and traffic cases, are dealt with by special magistrates. The Juvenile Court has jurisdiction to hear charges against children (aged under 14) and young persons (aged between 14 and 16) for any offence other than homicide. The Juvenile Court also has power to deal with care and protection cases involving young people aged up to.

4.4.3.6 Coroner's Court

Coroners are empowered to investigate deaths occurring in Hong Kong (and deaths occurring outside Hong Kong if the body is found within Hong Kong). Deaths are investigated if they are not certified by a doctor as being solely due to natural causes. Except when an individual dies in custody, or the Secretary for Justice directs, the decision whether or not to hold an inquest lies with the Coroners as does the decision whether or not to sit with a jury. However, where deaths occur in official custody, it is mandatory to sit with a jury. The purpose of an inquest is to ascertain the circumstances surrounding a particular death. If appropriate, Coroners may make recommendations designed to prevent a repetition of the fatality under investigation. There are three Coroners in the Coroner's Court.

4.4.3.7 The Labour Tribunal

Provides a quick, informal and inexpensive method of settling disputes between employees and employers. It deals with claims arising from the breach of a term of a contract of employment, for wages in lieu of notice of termination of service, arrears of wages, statutory holiday pay, annual leave pay, sickness allowance, maternity leave pay, bonus/double pay, severance pay, long service payments, etc. Legal representation is not allowed and hearings are informal. There is no upper limit on the amount of claim, but the Tribunal only hears cases which the amount of claim exceeds $8,000 for at least one of the claimants in a claim or which the number of claimants in the claim exceeds 10. Appeals may be brought to the Court of First Instance of the High Court on a point of law or jurisdiction. There are at present eight presiding officers with one Principal Presiding Officer.

4.4.3.8 The Small Claims Tribunal

Provides a quick, informal and inexpensive method of dealing with monetary claims involving amounts not exceeding $50,000. Legal representation is not allowed although the claimant may, with permission, authorize someone else (other than a lawyer) to appear as a representative. Appeals may be brought to the Court of First Instance of the High Court. There are at present six Adjudicators headed by a Principal Adjudicator.

4.4.3.9 The Obscene Articles Tribunal

Has two functions. Firstly, it has exclusive jurisdiction to determine whether an article is an obscene or indecent article and whether the matter publicly displayed is indecent. Secondly, the Tribunal has power to classify an article as Class I (neither obscene nor indecent Class II (an indecent article) or Class III (an obscene article). An author, printer, manufacturer, publisher, importer, distributor or owner of copyright of an article, may submit it to a tribunal for classification. There are two presiding magistrates in the tribunal. Each of them sits with two or more lay adjudicators selected from a wide panel of community representatives.

Chapter 5 ALTERNATE DISPUTE RESOLUTION (ADR)

5.1 INTRODUCTION

As the majority of stakeholder rely heavily on ADR to prevent or resolve claims and disputes. Frequently, multiple ADR techniques are designated by contract, with binding arbitration the forum of last resort if other techniques are unsuccessful. Litigation is simply too time consuming, costly and acrimonious for stakeholder.

The ADR techniques discussed in this chapter have been widely used and accepted by the industry as effective ways to promptly reach practical solutions to the myriad claims and disputes that are a reality on every project. These techniques can be used sequentially to provide a comprehensive blueprint for management of claims and disputes. The techniques include informal, quick and cost effective procedures, and, those escalating in cost, formality, time and the level of hostility to full-blown litigation.

The principal benefits of ADR are:

- Saves time;
- Saves legal expenses;
- Provides the parties an opportunity for greater control over the dispute resolution process;
- Allows parties to resolve their conflict in a more creative way than might be possible if it were left to a decision by a judge or jury;
- Gives the parties greater privacy in resolving their dispute than is afforded in a public courtroom;
- Reduces the emotional toll a lawsuit can take on everyone concerned; and
- Can permit valued relationships among the parties to be preserved.

Almost any means of resolving disputes without litigation could be described as an ADR technique. Any negotiation between parties would fall under this definition, since by its nature negotiation involves bringing the parties together to resolve a dispute. However, this chapter covers the formal ADR techniques typically used to resolve business disputes, such as mediation, arbitration and non-traditional techniques.

5.2 TYPE OF ALTERNATE DISPUTE RESOLUTION

5.2.1 Ombudsmen

Ombudsmen investigate and resolve complaints about public and private organizations. They also encourage good practice in the way complaints are handled by organizations and government bodies. The majority of recognized ombudsman schemes are set up by statute; others are voluntary non-statutory schemes set up on the initiative of the service sectors concerned. For example, services provided by insurance companies, banks and building societies are all covered by the Financial Ombudsman Service (FOS).

5.2.2 Conciliation

Conciliation involves an impartial third party helping the people in dispute to resolve their problem. The parties are free to agree to the resolution or not. In consumer disputes, conciliation is the first stage in the arbitration process and the conciliator is usually a member of the trade association.

5.2.3 Mediation

The most widely used method of dispute resolution in the industry. The most common misconception is that mediators settle disputes. They don't. Parties will settle a dispute as soon as they decide it is in their mutual best interests to do so. At the most basic level the mediator's function is to keep the parties talking and searching for ways to resolve the dispute. Mediation is a structured negotiation in which the mediator provides the structure. The mediator will establish ground rules and acts as a referee, facilitating communications between the parties.

Step 1: Individual Meeting

The service coordinator will arrange an introductory meeting with your mediators. The purpose of this meeting is to discuss your concerns and clarify the mediation process. The mediators will then help you to think about what you want, what other people might want, and how things could be improved. This initial meeting usually lasts" between" one hour and 90 minutes.

If during the course of the discussion you decide that you want to meet the other party the mediators will approach them on your behalf, but there will be no pressure for you to do so.

Step 2: Meeting Between the Other Party and the Mediators

The mediators approach the second party and ask them to participate in the mediation process. If they agree then we will make a convenient appointment. Of course they might not want to take part in the process and in this case you should discuss alternatives with your line manager, HR manager or union.

The second party will discuss their own concerns and feelings with mediators, who will again clarify the mediation process. The mediators treat everyone in exactly the same way and will not divulge details of these discussions unless they have permission to do so.

If everyone is willing to proceed at the end of this meeting we will schedule a joint meeting.

Step 3: Joint Mediation

Both parties take part in the joint session. The mediators will arrange to meet you and the other party before the session and will ensure you all enter the room at the same time. The mediators will run the session and accommodate comfort breaks, stopping the session if anyone feels uncomfortable.

This meeting will be an open and frank discussion of the issues, led by the mediator to ensure fairness and appropriate behavior. The mediator will start by explaining how the session will work, setting the agenda for the mediation and giving everyone uninterrupted time to put forward the key issues.

People often feel that progress is slow during the early stages and you should be prepared for periods of waiting. This is natural though and the mediation process will gather momentum as it comes closer to a conclusion.

Private meetings: During a joint meeting either party can ask to see the mediators privately. If this happens then both mediators will accompany them to a side room and ask the other party remains seated. Nothing said in a private discussion with one person will be repeated to the other without express permission.

Step 4: Concluding the Mediation Process

During the meetings, the mediators may take notes to help them remember the facts. You can see these notes at any time and they will be destroyed at the end of the session. If both parties feel more comfortable with a written agreement then we will provide one too.

The mediators will help the parties to draw up a simple statement outlining the key agreed areas. All parties will need to sign and date the agreement, which will also be signed by the mediators, and you can keep a copy for your records.

At the end of the meetings, the mediators will repeat that anything said or done during mediation cannot be discussed outside the meetings, unless both parties wish to discuss this with a manager.

Step 5: After Mediation

The mediators will contact all the parties after approximately three months to check how things are progressing. Our coordinator will send a feedback form to both parties to feed back on the mediator's performance and the service we provided. This information is confidential and will only be used to improve the mediation service.

5.2.4 Adjudication

Adjudication is where you and the other party appoint someone who is an expert in the subject to help resolve the dispute Adjudication can be used in any dispute, but is currently used almost exclusively in the construction and engineering industry. The adjudicator is usually a construction or engineering expert appointed to give an opinion on the issue to allow work to carry on. It's a more informal process than going to court. Some contracts include an adjudication clause, and if this is the case you have to use adjudication and comply with any decision made by the adjudicator. Adjudication is unlikely to help you if you wish to retain control over the solution to your dispute.

In mediation, a neutral facilitator works with the parties to assist them to reach their own solution. An adjudicator is usually an industry expert who makes technical decisions on the dispute which are generally binding on the parties.

The aim of adjudication is to resolve disputed issues in order to enable work to continue (either indefinitely or while awaiting the decision of a judge or arbitrator). Arbitration is a more formal process, and the arbitrator's decision is legally binding.

5.2.5 Early Neutral Evaluation

In Early Neutral Evaluation (ENE) an independent third party considers the claims made by each side and gives an opinion, either on the likely outcome or on a particular point of law. The opinion is non-binding; the parties can use it if they wish in considering how they want to proceed with their case. The opinion can be the basis for settlement. ENE can be particularly valuable to get an opinion on a point of law or to get a more realistic view of the chances of success at trial.

5.2.6 Expert Determination

In expert determination, an independent third party considers the claims made by each side and issues a binding decision. The third party is usually an expert in the subject of the dispute and is chosen by the parties, who agree at the outset to be bound by the expert's decision. It can be most suitable for determining technical aspects of a complex dispute. Expert determination is also a process of adjudication (see above), and parties agree at the outset to be bound by the expert's decision.

5.2.7 Med-arb

Med-arb is a combination of mediation and arbitration. Mediation is attempted first, and if no agreement results, the dispute will go to arbitration, where a binding decision will be issued. In some cases the same person acts as mediator and arbitrator; in others a different neutral is brought in to arbitrate.

5.2.8 Med-rec

Med-rec is a form of mediation in which the mediator gives the parties a recommendation for resolving the dispute. Mediation is conducted in the usual way, with the mediator encouraging the parties to reach their own agreed resolution. If they do not, they can ask the mediator to recommend a resolution. This recommendation can be accepted or not. If accepted by both parties it can become a binding settlement.

5.2.9 Arbitration

In arbitration an independent, impartial third party hears both sides in a dispute and makes a decision to resolve it. In most cases the arbitrator's decision is legally binding on both sides, so it is not possible to go to court if you are unhappy with the decision.

Arbitration is in many ways an alternative form of court with procedural rules which govern issues such as disclosure of documents and evidence. But arbitration is private rather than public. Hearings are less formal than court hearings, and some forms of arbitration do not involve hearings but are decided on the basis of documents only.

The process of arbitration differs among cases. The following is a list of the main steps in arbitration:

Initiating the Arbitration: A request by one party for a dispute to be referred to arbitration.

Appointment of Arbitrator: Arbitrators may be appointed by one of three ways: (1) directly by the disputing parties, (2) by existing tribunal members (For example, each side appoints one arbitrator and then the arbitrators appoint a third), (3) by an external party (for example, the court or an individual or institution nominated by the parties).

Preliminary Meeting: It is a good idea to have a meeting between the arbitrator and the parties, along with their legal counsel, to look over the dispute in question and discuss an appropriate process and timetable.

Statement of Claim and Response: The claimant sets out a summary of the matters in dispute as well as the proposed remedy to the respondent of what needs to be answered. It summarizes the alleged facts, but does not include the evidence through which facts are to be proved. The statement of response from the respondent is to admit or deny the claims. There may also be a counterclaim by the respondent, which in turn requires a reply from the claimant. These statements are called 'pleadings'. Their purpose is to identify the issues and avoid surprises.

Discovery and Inspection: These are legal procedures through which the parties investigate background information. Each party is required to list all relevant documents. This is called 'discovery'. Parties then 'inspect' the documents and agreed upon selection of documents for the arbitrator.

Interchange of Evidence: The written evidence is exchanged and given to the arbitrator for review prior to the hearing.

Hearing: The hearing is a meeting in which the arbitrator listens to any oral statements, questioning of witnesses and can ask for clarification of any information. Both parties are entitled to put forward their case and be present while the other side states theirs. A hearing may be avoided however, if the issues can be dealt with entirely from the documents.

Legal Submissions: The lawyers of both parties provide the arbitrator with a summary of their evidence and applicable laws. These submissions are made either orally at the hearing, or put in writing as soon as the hearing ends.

Award: The arbitrator considers all the information and makes a decision. An award is written to summarize the proceedings and give the decisions. The award usually includes the arbitrator's reasons for the decision.

Chapter **6** TERMS—(ALPHABETICALLY)

6.1 INTRODUCTION

This handy dictionary presents definitions and explanations that can be understood by Non-Legal Professionals. The terms are arranged in alphabetical order.

- You can achieve far better negotiated results if you have a good understanding of what contracts and their terminology actually mean
- You should never sign any contract unless you have read and understood what it aims to do and what the terminology means
- Improve the ability of managers to communicate with and instruct legal and contracts personnel
- Easy to carry with you
- Gives you a reason to look away from your computers

If you are the boss, or accountable for a contractual outcome, you must understand contracts and their meaning. When you understand what contracts mean you increase your control over the situation, your advisors, the other party, their advisors, and the negotiated outcomes.

Aa

Abandonment: Giving up a legal right.

Abate: To do away with a problem, such as a public or private nuisance.

Abatement: A reduction in some amount that is owed, usually granted by the person to whom the debt is owed. For example, a landlord might grant abatement in rent.

Abeyance: Temporary inactivity, to hold in suspension; a situation waiting to be settled.

Abet: To help someone commit a crime including helping them escape.

Abduction: Unlawful removal of a person (often a child) from their home environment.

Ab Initio: Being something done 'from scratch'. In legal parlance it stands from: 1. if any legal agreement is void ab initio then it stands null and void from the very beginning of its intended existence and not just from the instant its declared as void. 2. If a person enters onto someone's private property (real estate) by authority of law but later maltreats that authority then he becomes a trespasser ab initio.

Abscond: To secretly hide, conceal one, withdraw or depart.

Absolute Privilege: Privilege is a special legal right or immunity granted to a person or persons. Absolute privilege is immunity from lawsuit, usually a lawsuit for defamation, even if the action is wrong, malicious, or done with an improper motive. Absolute privilege is most often expressed for legislators.

Absolute Right: A right set out in the European Convention on Human Rights that cannot be interfered with lawfully, no matter how important the public interest in doing so might be. Absolute rights include freedom of thought, conscience, and religion and the prohibitions on torture, inhuman treatment or punishment, and *degrading treatment or punishment.

Absolute Title: Ownership of a *legal estate in registered land with a guarantee by the state that no one has a better right to that estate. An absolute title to freehold land is equivalent to an estate in fee simple in possession in unregistered land.

Abstract: A history of the ownership of a property, showing transfers in ownership and factors affecting ownership, such as mortgages.

Abstract of Title: A brief history of the titles for a piece of land. The abstract of title lists all of the legal actions that have been performed or used in conjunction with a piece of property. This is used to determine whether or not there is any kind of claim against a property.

Acceleration Clause: A clause in a contract that states that if a payment is missed, or some other default occurs (such as the debtor becoming insolvent), then the contract is fully due immediately.

Acceptance: The act of affirming an offer, either expressly or by implication through conduct, so as to enter into a contract. A contract is a legally binding agreement between two or more parties which starts with an offer from one person but which does not become a contract until the other party signifies an unequivocal willingness to accept the terms of that offer.

Accessory: A person who assists in the commission of a crime, as distinguished from the principal offender.

Accord and Satisfaction: An agreement between two or more persons or entities, which extinguish an obligation or settle a claim or law suit.

Account: An account is an oral or written detail of an event or situation. An account is an oral or written detail of an event or situation.

Accounts Receivable Financing: A continuing agreement by a bank, factor or other means of financing such as, to make a loan secured by its customer's receivables; to retain right of recourse for losses, and to advance funds on accounts without notice to borrower's customers.

Accommodation Endorser: A party who has put his or her name, without compensation, on commercial paper as a guarantor.

Accused: Charged with offense; as, an accused person.

Accretion: The imperceptible and gradual addition to land by the slow action of water.

Acknowledgment: Certification by a notary that the signature on the document was personally signed by the individual whose signature is affixed to the instrument.

Acquiescence: Action or inaction which binds a person legally even though it was not intended as such. For example, action which is not intended as a direct acceptance of a contract will nevertheless stand as such as it implies recognition of the terms of the contract. Acquiescence also refers to allowing too much time to pass since you had knowledge of an event which may have allowed you to have legal recourse against another, implying that you waive your rights to that legal recourse.

Acquit: to discharge, to find an accused "not guilty" after trial.

Act: 1. In general, any action by a person. 2. A statutory plan passed by Congress or any legislature which is a "bill" until enacted and becomes law. 3. For a court to make a decision and rule on a motion or petition, as in "the court will act on your motion for a new trial".

Action: In the law, a cause of action (sometimes called a claim) is a set of facts sufficient to justify a right to sue to obtain money, property, or the enforcement of a right against another party.

Actionable: Subject to and/or affording grounds for an action or lawsuit.

Act of Bankruptcy: An action of a debtor that shows an inability to pay their creditors or Debtor's action that may cause his or her creditors to petition courts to declare him or her bankrupt (in order to force a sale of the debtor's assets to satisfy their claims). In some jurisdictions, any failure to pay an obligation (above a certain amount) on due date may constitute an act of bankruptcy.

Act of God: An event which is caused solely by the effect of nature or natural causes and without any interference by humans whatsoever. Insurance contracts often exclude "acts of God" from the list of insurable occurrences as a means to waive their obligations for damage caused by hurricanes, floods or earthquakes, are considered "acts of God".

Actual cost: The cost of the work based on payment to the contractor for the actual time spent by the contractor's employees and subcontractors and the materials actually used.

Actusreus: The voluntary and wrongful act or omission that constitutes the physical components of a crime. Because a person cannot be punished for bad thoughts alone, there can be no criminal liability without actusreus.

Addendum: A document used to expand or more fully explain the terms of a solicitation which is incorporated as part of the original solicitation. This modification becomes a legal part of the solicitation. This term should not be confused with a contract amendment as it is not used to change the terms of a contract.

Addendum Bills: A term used to describe bills of quantities produced to modify the bills originally prepared.

Ademption: When property identified in a will cannot be given to a beneficiary because it no longer belonged to the deceased at the time of death. For example, the particular gift may have been destroyed, sold, lost due to debt in legal action or given away between the time of the will and the owners time of death.

Adhesion Contract: A fine –print consumer form contract which is generally given to consumers at point–of–sale, with no opportunity for negotiation as to its terms, and which, typically, sets out the terms and conditions of the sale to advantage the seller.

Adjournment: Putting off or postponing of proceedings; an ending or dismissal of further business by a court, legislature, or public official—either temporarily or permanently. If an adjournment is final, it is said to be sine die, "without day" or without a time fixed to resume the work. An adjournment is different from a recess, which is only a short break in proceedings.

Adjudication: The process of hearing and resolving a dispute before a court or administrative agency. It implies a final judgment based on the evidence presented, as opposed to a proceeding where the merits of the case were not considered by the court or administrative agency. **Adjuster:** A person who is employed to investigate and effect collection and settlement on an account.

Administration (Law): whereby an insolvent company can continue trading under supervision.

Administration Order: An order made in a county court for the administration of the estate of a judgment debtor. The order normally requires the debtor to pay his debts by installments: so long as he does so, the creditors referred to in the order cannot enforce their individual claims by other methods without the leave of the court. Administration orders are issued when the debtor has multiple debts but it is thought that his bankruptcy can be avoided.

Administrative Act: A decision, or refusal to make a decision, by an officer of a government department and which is subject to review either internally or externally by the courts.

Administrative Receiver: Official appointed by a court or a lender (under the terms of a secured debenture) who takes control of all, or substantially all, assets of a firm in receivership and is mandated to pay off the firm's debts, if possible, without liquidating it.

Administrator: One appointed to manage and distribute an estate where the decedent has not left a will, or when an executor has not been appointed or qualified under the will.

Admiralty Court: Court having jurisdiction over maritime financial and regulatory issues .

Admiralty Law: Body of orders, rules, and statutes concerning civil maritime financial and regulatory actions relating to ships and the sea, such as those arising out of collisions, financing of capital equipment, and international maritime treaties. It is administered by the admiralty courts.

AD Valorem Tax: The term ad valorem is derived from the Latin ad valentiam, meaning "to the value." It is commonly applied to a tax imposed on the value of property. Real property taxes that are imposed by the states, counties, and cities are the most common type of ad valorem taxes. ad valorem taxes can, however, be imposed upon Personal Property. For example, a motor vehicle tax may be imposed upon personal property such as an automobile.

Advanced Court Costs: Court costs include filing fees, charges for serving summons and subpoenas, court reporter charges for depositions, court transcripts and copying papers and exhibits. Court costs are often awarded to the successful party in a lawsuit.

Advance Payments: A payment situation whereby under certain circumstances it is possible to make a portion of the contract funds available to a provider prior to the delivery of services and or expenditure of funds by the provider.

Adversary Proceeding: A trial or other proceeding in which all have the opportunity to present their arguments: a proceeding involving a contested action.

Adverse Possession: Acquisition of title to real property owned by someone else, by open, notorious, and continuous possession for the statutory period of time. Burden to prove title is on the possessor, who does not have a marketable title until he obtains and records a judicial decree quieting title.

Adverse Witness: A witness who gives evidence unfavorable to the party who called him. If the witness's evidence is merely unfavorable he may not be impeached (*i.e.* his credibility may not be attacked) by the party calling him, but contradictory evidence may be called. If, however, the witness is *hostile he may be impeached by introducing evidence that shows his untruthfulness.

Advice on Evidence: The written opinion of counsel, usually prepared after*disclosure and inspection of documents, identifying the issues raised in the statements of case and advising counsel's instructing solicitor what evidence it will be necessary to call at the trial.

Advocate: An advocate is a term for a professional lawyer used in several different legal systems. These include Scotland, Belgium, South Africa, India, Scandinavian jurisdictions, Israel, and the British Crown dependencies of Jersey, Guernsey and the Isle of Man. The broad equivalent in many English law-based jurisdictions is "barrister".

Advocate General: An assistant to the judge of the European Court of Justice whose function is to assist the court by presenting opinions upon every case brought before it. The Advocate General acts as an amicus curiae in putting forward arguments based upon his own view of the interests of the European Union, although it is not open to any of the parties to the legal action to submit observations on his opinion.

Affiant: A person who makes and signs an Affidavit.

Affidavit: A statement sworn to and affirmed before an official who is authorized to administer oaths.

Affiliate: A business connected with another through common ownership and management.

Affirmation: A pledge that statements made are true which may be made in place of an oath if an oath is contrary to a person's religious belief or if the person has no religious belief. It can be used where a person is giving evidence in a court or where a declaration or affidavit is being made.

Affirmation of contract: 1. Action (or a failure to take action) performed with full knowledge of the facts, that establishes a contract as valid. For example, a buyer of goods affirms a purchase price by proceeding to resell them, or the seller of goods affirms a price by not taking any action when the buyer pays a certain sum in settlement of the invoice. 2. Continuation of a voidable contract by a contracting party instead of rescinding it (because of the other party's misrepresentation or other reason) or considering it discharged (because of the other party's breach of contract or other reason), with full knowledge of the facts. Such affirmation may be effected through an express declaration by a party to proceed with the contract, or it may be inferred from that party's conduct.

Affray: A fight between two or more persons in a public place so as to cause terror to the public.

Affreightment: A transportation contract whereby a transportation company, ship-owner or operator agrees to carry goods in return for a sum of money, the sum being paid called freight.

A Fortiori Argument: An argument from a strong source. This term is derived from the Latin legal maxim argumentum a fortiori. A fortiori argument is applied by following the logic that a point to be proved is followed from a stronger claim.

Agency: An agency is a collection agency that attempts to collect debts for creditors.

Agent: Somebody appointed to act on behalf of another person (known as the principal). The amount of authority to deal that the agent has is subject to agreement between the principal and the agent. However, unless told otherwise, third parties can assume the agent has full powers to deal.

Aggravated Damages: Damages awarded by a court to reflect the exceptional harm done to a plaintiff of a tort action.

Aggravating Factors: Are any relevant circumstances, supported by the evidence presented during the trial that makes the harshest penalty appropriate, in the judgment of the jurors.

Aggregation: Adding together the value of separate contracts for the same supply, works or service.

Aging of Accounts Receivable: A record of customers accounts receivable and how long they have remained unpaid beyond the terms of sale.

Agreement: A contact or arrangement for a consideration between two or more parties.

Agreement of Sale: A written agreement whereby the purchaser agrees to buy certain real estate and the seller agrees to sell upon terms and conditions set forth in the agreement.

Aid and Abet: To assist someone else to commit an offence without actually participating in the offence.

Aleatory Contract: A mutual agreement between two parties in which the performance of the contractual obligations of one or both parties depends upon a fortuitous event. The most common type of aleatory contract is an insurance policy in which an insured pays a premium in exchange for an insurance company's promise to pay damages up to the face amount of the policy in the event that one's house is destroyed by fire. The insurance company must perform its obligation only after the fortuitous event, the fire, occurs.

Alienation: The voluntary transfer of real property from one person to another.

Allegation: A statement of a party to an action, which sets out what he or she intends to prove or contend.

Alleged: Alleged describes some claim or something of which you should be wary and unconvinced.

Allonge: A piece of paper which has been attached to a contract, a check or any promissory note, on which to add signatures because there is not enough room on the main document.

ADR (Alternative Dispute Resolution):. ADR basically is an alternative to a formal court hearing or litigation. It is a collective term for the ways that parties can settle disputes, with (or without) the help of a third party. ADR are ways and methods of resolving disputes outside the judicial process (formal litigation – court).

Amend: To correct an error, modify, update or alter any legal document.

Amendment: A document by which significant changes are made to the terms of an executed contract. Changes requiring an amendment include, but are not limited to adjustments in costs, services, time period, and method of payment. The amendment is incorporated as part of the original contract.

Amenities: Tangible and intangible benefits generated and received through exercise of rights to real property, not necessarily in the form of money.

Amenity: Features, benefits or advantages of the local environment that people currently enjoy.

Amortization: Provision for the gradual reduction of an obligation by periodically contributing to a fund to discharge a debt or make replacement when it becomes necessary.

Animus Contrahendi: Latin: An intention to contract.

Annexation: The act of attaching, adding or joining one thing to another, generally a smaller or subordinate thing with a large or principal thing. Usually with respect to land or fixtures.

Annuity: A sum of money payable yearly.

Annul: Annul means to do away with, make null and void or reduce to nothing.

Answer: A written statement made by a defendant setting forth the grounds and reasons of his defense.

Antedate: A date entered on a legal contract or check that is prior to the actual date of occurrence. An antedate can sometimes be used if a contract has been delayed, to make sure the parties do not suffer from delays in the contract.

Antichresis: In the civil law, an antichresis is a contract for security between the debtor and his creditor; a transfer of possession of the pledged real property from the debtor to the creditor, including the fruits or rent income therefrom, in lieu of payments on the loan, including interest, for any such time period as is provided for in the contract. For the tenure of his occupation, the creditor has an obligation to maintain the real property in a state of good repair. The creditor does not become the owner of the real property.

Anticipatory Breach: when a party to a contract receives an indication from the other party that they intend on not performing their contractual obligations.

Anti-trust: The anti-trust laws apply to virtually all industries and to every level of business, including manufacturing, transportation, distribution, and marketing. They prohibit a variety of practices that restrain trade.

Appeal: To ask a more senior court or person to review a decision of a subordinate court or person. Appeals can continue all the way up to the Supreme Court, where the decision is final.

Appellant: A person who applies to a higher court for a reversal of the decision of a lower court.

Appearance: Coming into court as a party to a suit. Appearances are most often made by lawyers on their client's behalf. Any appearance by a lawyer binds the client. You can make a limited appearance called a "special appearance" to challenge the jurisdiction of the court.

Applicable Law Clauses: In its most basic form, the applicable law clause lays out exactly which state's laws the contract is governed by. For example: "This contract shall be governed by and construed under the laws of the UAE".

Application for Payment: The contractor's written request for payment. The Application for Payment itemizes the cost of the work in permanent place, as approved by the Owner's Representative, that has been completed in accordance with the contract documents.

Apportionment: The division and distribution of something into proportionate parts; to each according to their share.

Appraisal: A detailed assessment of the general capacity of a contractor, supplier or service provider to meet certain general criteria or standards or a written estimate and opinion of value; a conclusion resulting from the analysis of facts.

Appreciation: An increased conversion value of property or mediums of exchange due to economic or related causes which may prove to be either temporary or permanent.

Appropriation: 1. Allocation of payments to debts. In case of multiple loans, the payments can be applied against any debt, usually at the option of the debtor. In case of an open trade credit account, the law in general presumes that the first item on the credit side is intended to be applied against the first item on the debit side. 2. Assumption by a person of the rights of an owner with the intention of permanently depriving the owner of the subject property; theft.

Approved List: A list approved by the Council of potential contractors, suppliers or service providers, who have met pre-set criteria.

Appurtenance: Something that, although detached, stands as part of another thing. Used often in a real estate context where an "appurtenance" may be, for example, a right-of-way over water, which is part of the legal rights of the owner of another property.

Arbitration: Using an independent third party to settle disputes without going to court. The third party acting as arbitrator must be agreed by both sides. Contracts often include arbitration clauses nominating an arbitrator in advance.

Arraignment: In USA criminal law, the formal appearance of an accused person to hear, and to receive a copy of, the charge against him or her, in the presence of a judge, and to enter a plea of guilty or not guilty. The arraignment is the final preparatory step before a criminal trial.

Arrangement: A plan by a debtor for a settlement, satisfaction and/or an extension of time for payment of unsecured debts.

Arrears: A past due obligation; an unpaid account.

Arrest: To take into custody.

Arrest of Judgment: A motion by a defendant in criminal proceedings on indictment, between the conviction and the sentence, that judgment should not be given on the ground of some objection arising on the face of the *record, such as a defect in the indictment itself. Such motions are extremely rare in modern practice.

Articles of Agreement: Founding document of an entity. They set forth, among other provisions, the purpose and main powers of the entity, voting rights of members, and limitations. It is similar to articles of incorporation, but more commonly used to refer to the founding document of a non-profit organization.

As Is: Legal term used to disclaim some implied warranties for an item being sold.

Assent: A declaration of willingness to do something in compliance with a request.

Assess: To fix the rate or amount.

Assessable Income: Income on which liability to pay income tax is calculated.

Assessed Valuation: The value that a taxing authority places on real or personal property for the purpose of taxation.

Assessor: A person called in to assist a court in trying a case requiring specialized technical knowledge. The High Court and the Court of Appeal have wide powers to appoint assessors to assist them in any action, but this power is rarely exercised except in Admiralty cases. Assessors will not give oral evidence and will not be open to cross-examination or questioning.

Assets: Items on a balance sheet which represents the resources or property belonging to an individual or company of anything owned having a money value.

Assign: To give, to transfer responsibility, to another. An assignee is the person who receives the right or property being given and the assignor is the person giving.

Assignee: A person, to whom some right or property is assigned by another.

Assignment: A written contract for transfer of one's title, right or property to another.

Assignment for the Benefit of Creditors: A transfer to another by an insolvent debtor of any property real or personal for the payment of debts. This form of liquidation is generally simpler and usually offers greater dividends to creditors than does bankruptcy.

Assignor: Individual who transfers a title, claim, property, interest, or right to another person.

Assumpsit: Assumpsit is an express or implied agreement to perform an oral contract. An express assumpsit is where one undertakes verbally or in writing, not under seal, or on record, to perform an act, or to pay a sum of money to another an action to recover damages for breach of an express or implied contract or agreement that was not under seal. An implied assumpsit is where one has not made any formal promise to do an act or to pay a sum of money to another, but who is presumed from his conduct to have assumed an obligation to do the just and fair thing. Common or indebitatus assumpsit is brought for the most part on an implied promise. Special assumpsit is founded on an express promise or undertaking.

Attachment: Taking property into custody of the court, either to satisfy a judgment ultimately to be rendered or as a method of acquiring jurisdiction.

Attachment of Debt Orders: When creditors know that someone else owes you money they may apply to the court for an order. The court can order the person who owes you money to pay it to the creditor.

Attestation Clause: That clause wherein the witnesses certify that the instrument has been executed before them, and the manner of the execution of the same.

Attorney: A person admitted to practice law in at least one jurisdiction and authorized to perform criminal and civil legal functions on behalf of clients. These functions include providing legal counsel, drafting legal documents, and representing clients before courts, administrative agencies, and other tribunals.

Attorney Fees: The charge made by an attorney in the course of preparing and trying a law suit.

Attorney-in-Fact: A person, not necessarily a member of the Bar, yet authorized by another to act in his or her place. This authority is given by an instrument called a power of attorney.

Audi Alterampartem: (Latin: hear the other side) A principle of natural justice which requires that, where a decision may affect an individual's rights, that person has a right to be heard. It includes the right to receive notice of a hearing and to be legally represented.

Audit Trail: System or paper generated evidence showing how and why and by whom certain processes and functions were carried out.

Award: The issue of an order or contract to a supplier.

Bb

Bad Debt: An account receivable which is not collectible and charged off by creditors.

Bad Debt Reserve: An account to which doubtful or uncollectible receivables are charged.

Bad Faith: A person who intentionally tries to deceive or mislead another in order to gain some advantage.

Bail: The procedure which enables an accused person to be released from custody in between the date of being charged and the eventual hearing of the court case. Conditions can be specified, and a guarantor (surety) can be required.

Bailee: The person who receives property through a contract of bailment, from the bailor and who may be committed to certain duties of care towards the property while it remains in his or her possession.

Bailiff: A court official, usually a deputy sheriff, who keeps order in the courtroom and handles various errands for the judge and clerk.

Bailment: A delivery of goods from one person (the bailor) to another (the bailee) for some purpose, upon an express or implied contract that the goods will be redelivered to the bailor when that purpose has been fulfilled. A contract may be implied from the behaviour of the parties.

Balance of Probabilities: Burden of proof in civil trials.

Balloon Payment: A repayment of the outstanding principal sum made at the end of a loan period, interest only having been paid hitherto.

Bankrupt: A person who has legally declared bankruptcy.

Bankruptcy: The formal recognition that a person cannot pay their debts as they are due. Note this only applies to individuals, companies and partnerships that become insolvent are wound up.

Barrister: Specialist in litigation and advocacy who receives instructions from a solicitor. Barristers may not normally deal directly with members of the public.

Base Bid: The sum stated in a bid, as the base for which the bidder offers to perform the work described in the bidding documents, to which work may be added, or from which work may be deleted for sums stated in alternates.

Battle of the Forms: Two persons intending to contract but tendering differing form contracts rendering the conclusion as to the terms of the contract, or determination as to whether there was a contract, difficult.

Benchmarking: Comparison of performance against other providers of similar services, particularly those recognized as adopting best practice.

Bench: The Judge's seat or the judge, himself/herself, (*e.g.*, the attorney addressed the bench).

Bench Warrant: A legal process issued by a court for the arrest of a person for failure to obey a previous order of the court.

Beneficiary: A person who receives and benefits from the gifts or acts of another, such as one who is designated to receive the proceeds from a will or trust.

Bequeath: To leave personal property to another by will. To leave real property by will is to devise.

Best Alternative to a Negotiated Agreement ("BATNA"): A resistance level in negotiations corresponding to the best option outside the current relationship.

Best and Final Offer: The detailed and fully priced offer submitted by the respondent for the contract, following the issue of the Council's Invitation to submit best and final offer (BAFO) documentation. Where the Council accepts the offer it becomes legally binding on both parties.

Best Practice: The most effective and desirable method of carrying out a function or process derived from experience rather than theory.

Best Value: The highest overall value to the procuring agency based on objective factors determined by the procuring agency.

Beyond Reasonable Doubt: Beyond a reasonable doubt is the standard of proof that must be met in order to convict a criminal defendant of a crime. The judge will instruct a jury in all criminal trials that they can only find the defendant guilty if they are convinced "beyond a reasonable doubt" of his or her guilt. It is a stricter standard of proof than a "preponderance of the evidence," that is required to find in favor of a plaintiff in a civil case. Beyond a reasonable doubt is not capable of precise definition, but it doesn't require absolute certainty. It is sometimes referred to as "to a moral certainty".

Bias: An actual or potential decision-maker's predisposition for or against a party to a lawsuit or a particular group of people.

Bid: A complete and properly signed offer to do the work for the sums stipulated therein, submitted in accordance with the bidding documents.

Bidding Documents: Documents given to bidders to enable them to prepare a bid. Bidding documents consist of the Cover Page, Certification, Table of Contents, Advertisement for Bids or Request for Bid, Project Directory, Instructions to Bidders, Supplementary Instructions to Bidders, Information Available to Bidders, Bid Form, Bid Bond, Agreement, General Conditions, Supplementary Conditions, Exhibits, Specifications, List of Drawings, Drawings, and Addenda.

Bid Opening Clerk: The individual charged with the responsibility of receiving, logging, and opening bids.

Bifurcated Trial: A case in which the trial of the liability issue in a personal injury or wrongful death case is heard separate from and prior to trial of the damages in question.

Bilateral Contract: An agreement in which the parties exchange promises for each to do something in the future.

Bill of Costs: A written statement of the itemized taxable costs and disbursements.

Bill of Exchange: A written order, which may be negotiable or non-negotiable, directing one party to pay a certain sum of money to the drawer or to a third person.

Bill of Indictment: A formal written accusation charging someone with an*indictable offence. The usual method of preferring a bill of indictment (*i.e.*, bringing it before the appropriate court) is by committal proceedings before a magistrates' court.

Bill of Lading: Receipt and contract issued by a common carrier for the shipment of goods.

Bill of Particulars: A formal written statement setting forth an itemization of an account of which a claim and suit is brought.

Bill of Reduction: Generally where the tendered amount is greater than estimate, the technical officer may decide to delete specific items within the specification by initiating a bill of reduction to bring the tender sum in line with the estimate. The technical officer will prepare the bills of reduction, which will be issued by procurement to at least the lowest two tenderers.

Bill of Sale: A written instrument transferring title, right, and interest in personal property to another.

Binder: An agreement to cover an earnest money deposit for the purchase of real property as evidence of the purchaser's good faith and intention to complete the transaction.

Bind Over: To order a person to provide a bond or recognizance by means of which he guarantees to carry out some act (*e.g.* to appear in court at the proper time if he has been granted bail) or not to commit some offence (such as causing a breach of the peace).

Blanket Mortgage: This is the type of mortgage that covers more than one piece of property. If a borrower wants to purchase multiple properties they can all be financed into a blanket mortgage in order to avoid multiple closing cost and loan fees.

Blanket Order: A purchase order issued to purchase expendable items from a single vendor over a certain period of time, often being the fiscal year. Items are purchased under one purchase order rather than processing separate orders each time supplies are needed.

Blue-Pencil Severance: Striking out an offending part of a legal document, such as a contract or a statute.

Body of Deed: The operative parts of a deed which set out the term of agreement between the parties.

Boilerplate: Standard contract clauses use universal language as a type of template. Usually found at the end of a contract, boilerplate clauses include arbitration clauses, entire agreement clauses, and force majeure clauses.

Bonafide: In good faith. Usually implies an amount of trust that the parties are acting without any hidden motives. The opposite is mala fides — in bad faith.

Bona vacantia: Vacant property. Refers to a situation where property or goods end up not being owned by anyone. This can happen if a person dies without heirs or a company is struck off without all its property being distributed. It can also occur where a contract becomes void and property under it cannot be restored to an owner. In the UK, any such property then belongs to the Crown and expensive proceedings are required to get it back.

Bond: 1. A deed in which a person undertakes to do or refrain from doing certain things, *e.g.* good behavior bond. 2. Money paid to a landlord by a tenant at the start of a tenancy as security in case of future damage to premises or non-payment of rent.

Breach of Contract: Failure by one party to a contract to uphold their part of the deal. A breach of contract will make the whole contract void and can lead to damages being awarded against the party which is in breach.

Break Clause: A clause that allows a tenant to end a lease at specific times during the period of the lease.

Brief: A written document prepared by an attorney to serve as the basis of an argument upon a case in court.

Brown Clause: A contract term providing for liquidated prolongation costs is sometimes called a Brown Clause.

Bundle of Rights: Beneficial interests or rights which attach to the ownership of real property, including the right to sell, lease, encumber, use, enjoy, exclude, will, etc. When purchasing real estate, one actually buys the rights previously held by the seller, except those which are reserved or limited in the sale.

Burden of Proof: The obligation to prove what is alleged. In criminal cases, this obligation rests on the prosecution, which must prove its case beyond reasonable doubt. In civil cases, it rests on the plaintiff, who must prove his or her case on the balance of probabilities. Sometimes, however, this burden shifts, for example, where the defendant raises particular defenses.

By-laws: Bylaw (sometimes also spelled by-law or byelaw) can refer to a law of local or limited application, passed under the authority of a higher law specifying what things may be regulated by the bylaw, or it can refer to the internal rules of a company or organization. Former name of local laws.

Cc

Call for Tenders: A property owner's invitation, sometimes at large, sometimes to a select group, for bids to complete a particular project.

Call off Contract: A contract made following a formal tendering process with one or more contractors, suppliers or service providers for a defined range of works, goods or services covering terms and conditions (including price) which users 'call off' to meet their requirements.

Capacity to Contract: The legal competence of a person to enter into a valid contract. Usually the capacity to contract refers to the capacity to enter into a legal agreement and the competence to perform some act. The basic element to enter into a valid contract is that s/he much have a sound mind.

Capitalization: In appraising, determining value of property by considering net income and percentage of reasonable return on the investment.

Capitalization Rate: The percentage ratio between net income from investment and the value of the investment. Commonly expressed as "return on and return of" capital.

Case Evaluation/Early Neutral Evaluation: A process in which the parties summarize their case to an impartial "evaluator" who gives an opinion regarding the probable outcome if the case were litigated and renders a non-binding award as to the settlement value of the case. Case evaluation is used to encourage settlement and is particularly useful in resolving issues as to damages, when liability is not hotly contested.

Case Law: The law based on judicial opinions, including decisions that interpret statutes, rather than law based on statutes and other sources.

Cash Value: The amount available in cash upon cancellation of an insurance policy, usually a whole life policy, before it becomes payable upon death or maturity. also called cash surrender value or surrender value.

Causa Causans: The primary cause or the originator of an action. It is the foundation of all the causes. It refers to the immediate cause that resulted in the damage. To get the damages the claimant must prove that the defendant's breach of duty caused the harm. But the defendant need not prove the original cause of the harm. However while determining the question of harm the court will consider if the defendant has given explanation as to the original cause of the harm.

Causation: The cause and effect relationship between an act or omission and damages alleged in a tort or personal injury action.

Caveat: A notice given to an appropriate officer ordering him or her not to take a certain step until the person giving the notice (the caveator) has had an opportunity to object (*e.g.* to a transfer of land).

Caveat Emptor: Buyers beware. This is a general rule that it is up to the buyer to find out if what they are buying is what they want. Consumer regulations require certain information to be disclosed to consumers and insurance contracts are covered by the uberrimae fides—but many types of business contracts are covered by the caveat emptor rule.

Certainty of Terms: A legal requirement of a valid offer to contact; that it must be precise and definite in order to be subject to acceptance.

Certificate for Payment: A written instrument issued by the Owner's Representative upon receipt of a contractor's Application for Payment. The Certificate for Payment is issued to the University and authorizes payment to the contractor for the amount the Owner's Representative determines to be properly due.

Certificate of Pending Litigation: A registration or/of a notice or warning that litigation is ongoing as to ownership of a particular piece of land or other real property.

Certificate of Title: A document stating that title to a particular property is clear. It is prepared by an attorney or qualified person who has examined the abstract of title, but is not to be confused with title insurance. It is only an opinion that title is good. Usually given to a home owner with the deed.

Certiorari: A writ issuing from a superior court calling up the record of a proceeding in an inferior court for review.

Change Order: A post-award modification to a construction contract. A change order may clarify, revise, add to, or delete previous requirements of the work, adjust the contract sum, or adjust the contract time.

Chattel: Personal property which is tangible and movable. (The word "chattel" evolved from the word "cattle", one of man's early important possessions.)

Chirograph: A medieval form of contract which allowed for several verifiable authentic versions.

Choice of Law Clause: A term of a contract which sets the jurisdiction for dispute resolution, or the applicable law, in the event of any dispute between the contracting parties.

CIF: Transportation contract acronym for "cost, insurance and freight" usually in reference to the sale price being inclusive thereof.

Circumstantial Evidence: Evidence of one fact from which another fact can be inferred. Circumstantial evidence is less persuasive than direct evidence. For instance, the 50 feet of skid marks left by an automobile preceding the point of impact with a school bus is circumstantial evidence of the automobile's speed based on the direct evidence of the actual skid marks on the roadway.

Citation: A writ issued by a court ordering a person to appear at a specific time and place and, at that time and place, do a specific act or to show the court sufficient cause why he or she cannot do so or should not be required to do so. See show cause order.

Citizen's Arrest: An arrest by any person who is not a police officer or who does not have a warrant to arrest.

Civil Action: Legal action brought to enforce, redress or protect private rights. All proceedings except criminal proceedings.

Civil Code: A document in civil law jurisdictions that purports to be a compendium of the applicable law as it pertains to the citizen.

Civil Commotion: Lord Mansfield defines a civil commotion to be "an insurrection of the people for general purposes, though it may not amount to rebellion where there is an usurped power.

Civil Law: Civil law seeks to resolve non-criminal disputes such as disagreements over the meaning of contracts, property ownership, divorce, child custody, and damages for personal and property damage. A civil court is a place where people can solve their problems with people peacefully. The function of civil law is to provide a legal remedy to solve problems. Sometimes civil law is based on a state or federal statute; at other times civil law is based on a ruling by the court.

Civil Liability: A civil law requirement to compensate another because of an unlawful injury to his/her person or property.

Civil Liberties: Natural rights which appertain and are inherent to each person as a human being, and which are protected.

Civil Right Assurance: Assurance that no person will be discriminated against or excluded from operations, programs or activities on the basis of race, color, age, sex, religion, handicap or national origin.

Claim: A demand for payment and or an account placed for collection by a creditor.

Claimant: A person applying for relief against another person in an action, suit, petition, or any other form of court proceeding. Before the introduction of the*Civil Procedure Rules in 1999, a claimant was called a plaintiff.

Claim form (in Civil Proceedings): A formal written statement setting out details of the claimant: defendant, .and the remedy being sought. The claim form may also contain details of the claim (the particulars of claim); alternatively, these can be served separately. Since the introduction of the Civil Procedure Rules in 1999, the usual method of initiating civil proceedings is by issuing a claim form; all previous methods (*e.g.* writ of summons, originating summons) have now been rendered obsolete.

Clause: A sub-division of a document. A clause of a written contract contains a term or provision of the contract. Clauses are usually numbered consecutively (1, 2,etc.); sub clauses may follow a clause, numbered 1.1, 1.1.1, etc.

Client: A person or firm who engages the professional advice or services of another.

Clear Title: A title free and clear of all encumbrances.

Closed-shop Agreement: A collective agreement requiring members of a particular group of employees to be or become members of a specified trade union.

Close of Pleadings: Formerly, a stage in the course of pleading in an action in the High Court that occurred 14 days after service of the reply, defense to counterclaim, or defense. This stage has been taken over by the functions of case management and track allocation.

Closing Statement: Closing statement is the attorney's final statement to the judge or jury in a trial. It is the concluding statement of each party's counsel and is made before deliberation begins.

Cloud on Title: An apparent claim or encumbrance, such as a lien, that, if true, impairs the right of the owner to transfer his or her property free and clear of the interests of any other party.

Code of Practice: A set of guidelines for fair practice developed for a specific industry or occupation. May be voluntary or statutory.

Codicil: A document signed by a will maker that alters or adds to an existing will.

Collateral Contract: A subsidiary contract that induces a person to enter into a main contract. For example, if X agrees to buy from Y goods made by Z, and does soon the strength of Z's assurance as to the high quality of the goods, X and Z may beheld to have made a collateral contract consisting of Z's promise as to quality given in consideration of X's promise to enter into the main contract with Y.

Collateral Heir: One who is not in the direct line of the deceased, but from a collateral line, as a brother/sister, aunt/uncle, nephew/niece or cousin of the deceased.

Collateral Security: A separate obligation attached to a contract to guarantee its performance; the transfer of property or of other contracts or valuables, to ensure the performance of a principal agreement.

Collective Agreement: term used for agreements made between employees and employers, usually involving trade unions. They often cover more than one organization. Although these can be seen as contracts, they are governed by employment law, not contract law.

Collective Bargaining Agreement: A contract on hiring, working conditions and dispute resolution between an employer and a union, the latter representing employees of a defined group.

Collusion: A fraudulent arrangement between two or more parties whereby prices or service requirements are manipulated to get round competitive tendering.

Color of Title: The appearance of title (also called "apparent title"). Any fact, extraneous to the act or will of the claimant, which appears, on its face, to support his claim of title but, because of defect, falls short of establishing title.

Closed-shop Agreement: A collective agreement requiring members of a particular group of employees to be or become members of a specified trade union.

Consensus ad Idem: Agreement on an idea. This is the concept that the parties to the contract must all be in agreement on the basis of the contract. If it is discovered that the parties were thinking different things, then there is no consensus and the contract is void.

Consortium: An unincorporated group of firms or individuals, often formed to tender for a contract with a view to forming a company or working in some other way in the event of winning.

Comfort Letters: Documents issued to back up an agreement but which do not have any contractual standing. They are often issued by a parent or associate company stating that the group will back up the position of a small company to improve its trading position. They always state that they are not intended to be legally binding.

Commitment of Funds: Reservation of funds prior to obligation for a specific purpose, based on an estimate.

Committal proceedings: Where a Magistrates' Court hears evidence on an indictable charge and decides whether the accused should be sent for trial (also called a preliminary examination).

Common Element: In a condominium, land and parts of buildings used by all owners for mutual convenience and safety. See Condominium.

Common Expense: In a condominium, expenses of operation and sums declared by the bylaws to be common expense.

Common Law: Judge-declared law. Law which exists and applies to a group on the basis of customs and legal precedents developed over hundreds of years in Britain.

Community Property: Property accumulated through joint efforts of husband and wife, or by either one, during their marriage and owned in common.

CTO (Community Treatment Order): Treatment of an involuntary patient by a medical practitioner in the community, not in a mental hospital.

Community Visitor: A person with authority to monitor and report on the performance of mental health services and the welfare of their patients.

Company Seal: An embossing press used to indicate the official signature of a company when accompanied by the signatures of two officers of the company. Since 1989 it has been possible for a company to indicate its agreement without use of the seal, by two signatures (directors or company secretary) plus a formal declaration. However, some companies still prefer to use a seal and the articles of a company can override the law and require a seal to be used.

Comparable: Properties listed in appraisal reports which are substantially equivalent to the subject property, comparable in selling price, rental, income or similar measure.

Compensable Interest: Interest of parties that is to be compensated.

Compensatory Damages: Damages that compensate the injured victim for injuries actually endured.

Competency: Legal capacity to testify, determined by: 1. An understanding of the obligation to tell the truth, 2. Ability to communicate, and 3. A knowledge of the topic of the testimony.

Competitive Tendering: Awarding contracts by the process of seeking competing bids from more than one firm.

Complainant: A person who begins a prosecution against another in the Magistrates' Court, a plaintiff.

Compound Interest: Interest paid both on the original principal and on interest accrued from the time it fell due.

Comprehensive Insurance: Insurance that covers claims against the insured by other persons for damage to their property as well as covering the insured for damage to his or her own property.

Compromise: An adjustment or arrangement by mutual consent, for settlement of an account or dispute.

Compulsory Third Party Insurance: Insurance paid with vehicle registration to insure against damage caused to other people, limited to personal injuries suffered by them.

Concealment: An act intended or known to be likely to keep another party from learning a fact.

Concession: A privilege granted to an individual by the Government, to sell food, etc., on Government land.

Condemnation: In real property law, the process by which property of a private owner is taken for public use, with just compensation to the owner. Condemnation occurs under the right of eminent domain.

Conciliation: Process of resolving disputes which involves negotiations between parties, assisted by a conciliator. Conciliation aims for mutual agreement rather than a decision in favour of one side.

Conditions: Major terms in a contract. Conditions are the basis of any contract and if one of them fails or is broken, the contract is breached. These are in contrast to warranties, the other type of contract term, which are less important and will not usually lead to the breach of the contract-but rather an adjustment in price or a payment of damages.

Condition Precedent: A contractual condition that suspends the coming into effect of a contract unless or until a certain event takes place.

Condition Subsequent: A condition which, if it occurs, will defeat an existing estate in real estate or terminate an existing obligation.

Conditional Commitment: A commitment for a loan subject to one or more conditions.

Conditional Commitment Sale: A contract whereby the owner retains title to the property until the purchaser has met all of the terms and conditions of the contract.

Condominium: Fee ownership of a unit in multi-unit building with joint ownership of common areas.

Confidentiality: Protection against disclosure to an outside person of information revealed in a professional relationship, *e.g.*, doctor-patient.

Confidentiality Agreement: An agreement made to protect confidential information if it has to be disclosed to another party. This often happens during negotiations for a larger contract, when the parties may need to divulge information about their operations to each other. In this situation, the confidentiality agreement forms a binding contract not to pass on that information whether or not the actual contract is ever signed. Also known as a non-disclosure agreement.

Conflict of Interest: A situation where a person's own interests, or a duty towards someone else, may affect the way they carry out a duty towards others.

Consensus Ad Idem: An agreement—a meeting of the minds between the parties where all understand the commitments made by each. A basic requirement for a contract.

Consent: Agreement to an action or arrangement. See also: informed consent.

Consideration: In a contract each side must give some consideration to the other. Often referred to as the quid pro quo —see the Latin terms below. Usually this is the price paid by one side and the goods supplied by the other. But it can be anything of value to the other party, and can be negative – *e.g.*, someone promising not to exercise a right of access over somebody else's land in return for a payment would be a valid contract, even if there was no intention of ever using the right anyway.

Consignment: An arrangement whereby the consignor (seller) remains the owner of the property until such time as the consignee (buyer) sells the goods; at which time the consignee generally holds the proceeds of the sale in trust for the benefit of the consignor.

Consortium: An unincorporated group of organizations or individuals, often formed to tender for a contract with a view to working together.

Constructive Eviction: Breach of a covenant of warranty or quiet enjoyment; for example, the inability of a purchaser or lessee to obtain possession by reason of a paramount outstanding title. An act by the landlord which deprives the tenant of the beneficial use and occupancy of the premises devised.

Constructive Notice: Often called legal notice, the conclusive presumption that all persons have knowledge of the contents of a recorded instrument.

Consul: A representative of a foreign government assigned to another country to promote and protect the commercial interests of the subjects of his government.

Consumer: A person who buys goods or services but not as part of their business. A company can be a consumer for contracts not related to its business—especially for goods or services it buys for its employees. Charities are also treated as consumers.

Consumer Lease: A contract for hire of goods by a person for a specified period and rental.

Contact Order: An order stating the kind and frequency of contact between a child and another person—usually the parent with whom the child is not living. Now called a parenting order.

Contempt of Court: The failure to obey a court order or an act which shows a disregard for the authority of the court or judge. A person in contempt may face imprisonment.

Continuance: The adjournment or postponement of an action pending in court.

Contract: An agreement, either oral or written to do or not to do certain things. In real estate, there are many different types of contracts, including listings, contracts of sale, options, mortgages, assignments, leases, deeds, escrow agreements, and loan commitments, among others.

Contract Administration: The management of all actions after the award of a contract that must be taken to assure compliance with the contract; *e.g.*, timely delivery, acceptance, payment, closing contract, etc.

Contract Closeout: The final process or steps to be taken upon completion or termination of a contract. This may include, but is not limited to: 1. processing the final payment; 2. recovering any overpayment; or 3. recovering equipment purchased and to be returned in accordance with the terms of the contract.

Contract Default: The failure to perform or meet contract terms and conditions.

Contract Duration: The length of time for which a contract is legally binding on both parties. It is normally specified in the contract under "effective starting" and "ending" dates.

Contract Documents: Documents incorporated in the enforceable agreement between the Council and the contractor, including contract conditions, specification, pricing document, form of tender and the successful tenderers responses (including method statements), and other relevant documents expressed to be contract documents (such as correspondence, etc.)

Contract File: The official record for the procuring agency which must be maintained for a period of five (5) years following contract closeout or resolution of pending action (*e.g.*, legal, audit, etc.) whichever is later.

Contract Hire: An 'Off Balance Sheet' funding method where a company hires a vehicle from for a specified period and makes regular payments. The leasing company retains ownership of the vehicle and is responsible for the associated risks. At the end of the contract period the vehicle is returned to the leasing company.

Contract Note: A certificate confirming the terms of a sale of specified assets or securities between two parties.

Contract Number: A unique number assigned to each contract.

Contract Purchase: Generally an 'On-Balance-Sheet' funding method where a company hires a vehicle for a specified period and makes regular payments. The difference to Contract Hire is that the company/driver has the ability to purchase the car at the end of the contract for a predetermined amount (balloon figure) as long as the 'Sales Agency Agreement' has been completed.

Contract Race: A contract race will arise where a seller decides to deal with more than one prospective buyer, with a view to exchanging contracts with whichever buyer is ready to do so first.

Contract Renewal: Contracts for commodities or contractual services may be renewed. Renewal of a contract shall be by mutual consent in writing and shall be subject to the same terms and conditions set forth in the initial contract.

Contract Rent: Payment for use of property, as specified in a lease.

Contract Sum: An agreed lump sum to be paid for the whole of the Services, usually in installments according to a Payment Schedule.

Contract Time: The number of days set forth in the Agreement within which full completion of the work must be achieved. The contract time may be adjusted only by change order.

Contract Value: The total monetary value of a contract over its full duration (not annual value).

Contractor: An organization or individual who has made a contract to undertake works, supply goods or provide services.

Contravene: To breach, neglect or refuse to comply with a particular requirement or condition.

Contributory Negligence: A defense in an action for damages for injuries arising from the defendant's negligence. The defendant attempts to prove that the plaintiff's own negligence caused or contributed to the injuries suffered.

Contributory Negligence: A person's carelessness for his own safety or interests, which contributes materially to damage suffered by him as a result partly of his own fault and partly of the fault of another person or persons. Thus careless driving, knowingly travelling with a drunken driver, and failure to wear a seat belt are common forms of contributory negligence in highway accidents. The effect of contributory negligence is to reduce the claimant's damages by an amount that the court thinks just and equitable.

Concurring Opinion: A judge's opinion that agrees with the result of the majority of the court but disagrees with the reasons the majority used to support that result.

Conventional Mortgage: A mortgage on real estate securing a loan made by a private investor, not guaranteed by a Government agency.

Conveyance: The transfer of title to real property by means of a written instrument, such as a deed.

Cooling off Period: The time during which a purchaser can withdraw from a contract after signing.

Copyright: The rights belonging to the owner or licensee of literary, artistic and dramatic works, films and sound recordings, to reproduce, perform or otherwise deal with these works.

Corporal Punishment: Any physical punishment, usually one causing pain.

Corporation: A company; a business with Limited (Ltd) or Proprietary Limited (Pty Ltd) after its name.

Corroborate: To strengthen; to add weight by additional evidence.

Corroboration: Evidence that confirms the accuracy of other evidence "in a material particular". In general, English law does not require corroboration and any fact may be proved by a single item of credible evidence. The obligation to warn the jury of the dangers of acting on uncorroborated evidence of accomplices or of complainants in cases of sexual offences has been abolished: the judge now has a discretion to indicate the dangers of a jury relying on particular evidence. Corroboration remains mandatory in cases of treason and *perjury and for opinion evidence as to some matters, *e.g.*, speeding.

Cosigner: Another individual who signs for a loan and assumes equal liability for the debt.

Cost Plus Incentive Fee Contract (CPIFC): A type of contract where the buyer reimburses the seller for the seller's allowable costs and the seller earns a profit if defined criteria are met.

Cost Plus: The method of payment for contracts for which tenderers quote a lump sum or % addition to their costs (which would be reimbursed).

Cost Reimbursement Type Contracts: A category of contracts based on payments to a Contractor for allowable estimated costs, normally requiring only a 'best efforts' performance standard from the Contractor. Risk for all growth over the estimated value rests with the project owner.

Counter Claim: A counter claim is a claim made by a defendant in response to the claimant's claim. Counter claims are usually made in conjunction with the defence in the legal proceedings.

Counter Offer: A reply to an offer which is conditional.

Court Martial: A military court set up to try and punish offences committed by members of the army, navy or air force.

Covenant: A written agreement in a deed which pledges that either party will perform or abstain from specified acts on a certain property, or which specifies or forbids certain uses of the property.

Conveyance: A written document which transfers property from one person to another, usually real property.

Cover Note: A document provided by an insurer as evidence of temporary insurance cover before a formal policy is issued.

Credit: The promise to pay in the future in order to buy or borrow in the present; a sum of money due a person or business.

Credit Contract: A written agreement between the creditor and debtor that enforces the terms of the contract.

Credit history: A record of how a person has repaid debts.

Credit Line: The assignments to each account of a credit limit which indicates the maximum amount of credit to be extended.

Credit Rating: An evaluation by a creditor or credit reporting agency to reflect a debtor's credit history based on payment pattern.

Credit Reporting Agency: A company that keeps credit records on individuals.

Creditor: An individual or business who makes credit available by lending money or selling goods and services for credit.

Criminal Negligence: Reckless disregard for the lives or safety of other persons.

Critical Path: The optimum sequence of work activities which, if delayed or extended, will delay the scheduled completion of one or more of the milestones specified in the contract schedule, the scheduled completion of the work, or both.

Cross-Complaint: An action brought by a party sued against the party who sued or against a third party.

Cross Examination: The examination of a witness who has already testified in order to check or discredit the witness's testimony, knowledge, or credibility.

Curtilage: The yard surrounding a residence or dwelling house which is reserved for or used by the occupants for their enjoyment or work.

Custody: Charge and control of a person or item of property.

Custom: The consensual regulation of human conduct and commerce by the community itself.

Cy-pres: (French term meaning) "as close as possible." When a gift is made by will or trust and it is no longer possible to follow the instructions of the donor, a judge, estate, or trustee may apply the Cy Pres doctrine to fulfil the donor's wishes as nearly as possible. It is usually applied in the case of a gift made for charitable or educational purposes when the named recipient of the gift does not exist, has dissolved or no longer conducts the activity for which the gift is made.

Cyber-bullying: Using the Internet to support deliberate, repeated and hostile behaviour by an individual or group that is intended to harm someone else.

Cyberspace: Synonymous with Internet; a decentralised but interconnected body of data and self-maintained telecommunications network.

Cybersquatting: The bad faith registration of trademarks, as domain names, by non-trademark owners, who then try to sell the domain names back to the trademark owners.

Dd

Damages: Money paid as the normal remedy in the law as compensation for an individual or company's loss. If another type of remedy is wanted (such as an injunction - see general contract terms below) but cannot be or is not given by the court, then damages will be awarded instead.

Debenture: A formal debt agreement. It refers to both the agreement and the document that verifies it. It is usually issued by companies and is generally supported by security over some property of the debtor. If the debtor defaults, the creditor can take and sell the property. Debentures are often transferable, so the creditor can sell it and there are markets on formal stock exchanges that deal in types of debenture. It is sometimes referred to as debenture stock. A mortgage is a type of debenture but one that is always secured, usually against land.

Debt Agreement: An arrangement for dealing with unpaid debts that is less formal and intrusive than bankruptcy.

Debtor: A person who owes a debt.

Debt Securities: Debts which can be bought and sold, such as debentures.

Debt Service: Periodic payment on a debt, for interest on and retirement of the principal.

Deceit: When one person deliberately misleads a second person with a statement which causes the second person to do something that causes them damage.

Deceptive Trade Practice: An intentional act or omission in the course of trade or commerce that has the tendency or capacity to mislead or create the likelihood of deception.

Declaratory Judgment: A judgment that merely states the court's opinion on a question of law or declares the rights of the parties, without normally including any provision for enforcement. A claim for declaration may, however, be combined with one for some substantive relief, such as damages.

Declaratory Order: A formal statement by a court to clarify a specific point of law for interested parties.

Decree: An order by a court.

Decree Absolute: The final court order which ends a marriage.

Decree nisi: A provisional court order which orders that a marriage should be dissolved.

Deed: A legal instrument in writing, duly executed, sealed, and delivered, whereby the owner of real property (guarantor) conveys to another (grantee) some right, title, or interest in real estate.

Deed of Arrangement: A written agreement which can be made, when a debtor is in financial trouble, between the debtor and the creditors. It is intended to benefit the creditors and avoid the bankruptcy of the debtor. The creditors get a proportion of the money owing to them.

Deed Restriction: A provision in a deed controlling or limiting the use of the land.

De Facto: De Facto is a legal term meaning "in fact" or "in reality", which is used to qualify many legal terms.

Defamation: making a statement, either orally or in writing, which damages someone's reputation.

Default: Failure to perform a specific, required legal duty.

Default Judgment: A judgment granted when the defendant fails to respond or appear in court for hearings of any kind.

Defeasance: A side-contract which contains a condition which, if realized, could defeat the main contract.

Defence: The name for the team of people (lawyers and so on) against proceedings brought against someone. It is also in a civil case a written statement (pleading) by the defendant setting out the facts that the defence will rely on.

Defendant: A person who has been charged with a criminal offence or whom a civil action has been brought against.

Deferred Maintenance: Existing but unfulfilled requirements for repairs and rehabilitation, deferred until a later date.

Deficiency Judgment: At a foreclosure sale, the difference between the indebtedness sued upon and the sale price or market value of the real estate. See also Deficiency Payment.

Deficiency Payment: Additional compensation required in a final judgment in condemnation proceedings. See also Deficiency Judgment.

De Jure: In law. According to law, the opposite of de facto.

Delegation: Allowing lower ranking officials to make decisions on behalf of the person responsible by law for making the decision. Also: to delegate.

Delivery Method: A term used to describe the process by which a capital improvement project proceeds from concept, through design and construction, to occupancy. Delivery methods include the following: Conventional (design-bid-build), Fast-track, Design-build, Turnkey, Lease-back, Other (These include joint ventures, leasing, tenant improvements, and purchase of developer-owned projects.)

Delusion: A firm yet irrational belief and which may affect an individual's capacity to contract

Demand Letter: A letter from a lawyer, on behalf of a client, that demands payment or some other action, which is allegedly due or in default.

Demonstrative Evidence: Actual objects, models and other devices which are supposedly intended to clarify the facts for the judge.

Denial: A legal form of pleading, refusing to admit the truth of a statement, charge, and so forth.

De Novo: The Latin word for "new." When an appeals court hears a case de novo, it looks at the record as if for the first time, and applies the same standards that the lower court used.

Deponent: Someone who gives evidence or acts as a witness. The testimony of a deponent is written and carries the deponent's signature.

Deportation: Expulsion from a country of a resident non-citizen who has committed a serious crime or is considered a threat to national security.

Depositions: The final determination by a court in a lawsuit or criminal charge.

Determination: Decision. In legal use, determination usually implies the conclusion of a dispute or lawsuit by the rendering of a final decision. After consideration of the facts, a determination is generally set forth by a court of justice or other type of formal decision maker.

Deterioration: Impairment of condition. One of the causes of depreciation and reflecting the loss in value brought about by wear and tear, disintegration, use in service, and the action of the elements.

Dictation: Situation where a decision-making body improperly allows itself to be directed by another person or body when making a decision.

Dilapidation: A state of disrepair. The term is usually used in relation to repairs required at the end of a lease or tenancy.

Direct Contempt: Contempt of Court which is aimed expressly against the dignity or authority of the Court itself in the person of its judges or officers.

Directed Verdict: A ruling by a judge typically made after the plaintiff has presented all of its evidence but before the defendant puts on its case that awards judgment to the defendant. A directed verdict is usually made because the judge concludes the plaintiff has failed to offer the minimum amount of evidence to prove the case even if there were no opposition. In other words, the judge is saying that, as a matter of law, no reasonable jury could decide in the plaintiff's favor. In a criminal case, a directed verdict is a judgment of acquittal for the defendant.

Direct Evidence: Evidence tendered in trial in the form of recounting of personal observations or a document which directly establishes a fact sought to be proven.

Directions Hearing: A hearing held before the full hearing so that the court or tribunal can give directions to the parties about how the action should proceed.

Directory: (A provision) that does not have to be strictly complied with; not mandatory.

Disbursement: Money paid out on behalf of another. In a solicitor's bill, a disbursement may include payments made on lodging documents, and stamp duty, for example.

Discharge: To fulfill or be released from an obligation. A debt is discharged when it is paid.

Disclosure: Giving particular information to another party as required by a contract or legal process.

Discovery: A procedure by which documents relevant to a civil action are exchanged between the parties before the case comes on for hearing.

Disclaimer: A written document denying legal responsibility, or a limitation of rights that might otherwise be claimed.

Discretion: Power to choose whether to do or not to do a certain thing, *e.g.* investigate a complaint.

Dishonor: Failure to make a payment of a negotiable instrument on its due date.

Dismissal: An order terminating the case prior to its normal end.

Dismissal without Prejudice: A dismissal of a case based on a procedural error. The case can be filed again so long as the procedural error is corrected in the amended action.

Dissolution of A Corporation: Termination by surrender or forfeiture of its charter by proceedings for winding up its operations under law and ending its existence.

Distribution: One or more dividend payments made to creditors who have approved claims filed in a bankruptcy, assignment or receivership.

Dividend: A sum of money paid and distributed to shareholders of a corporation or creditors of an insolvent business.

Dock Brief: The obsolete procedure by which a defendant to a criminal charge could, on indictment, select any barrister in the court who was not otherwise engaged to represent him, on payment of a nominal fee.

Docket: An official court record book which lists all the cases before the court and which may also note the status or action required for each case.

Docketing the Appeal: The court's formal recording of the filing of an appeal by one of the parties to the lawsuit. An appeal is a legal action which seeks review by a court of a lower court's decision.

Documentary Evidence: Evidence contained in or on documents can be a form of real evidence. For example, a contract offered to prove the terms it contains is both documentary and real evidence. When a party offers a document into evidence, the party must authenticate it the same way as any other real evidence, either by a witness who can identify the document or by witnesses who can establish a chain of custody for the document.

Document of Title to Goods: A document, such as a *bill of lading, that embodies the undertaking of the person holding the goods (the bailee) to hold the goods for whoever is the current holder of the document and to deliver the goods to that person in exchange for the document.

Doctrine of Precedent: The policy of courts to abide by or adhere to principles established by decisions in earlier cases.

Domicile: The country that a person treats as his permanent home and to which he has the closest legal attachment. A person cannot be without a domicile and cannot have two domiciles at once. He acquires at birth a domicile of origin. Normally, if his father is then alive, he takes his father's domicile; if not, his mother's. He retains his domicile of origin until (if ever) he acquires a domicile of choice in its place. A domicile of choice is acquired by making a home in a country with the intention that it should be a permanent base. It may be acquired at any time after a person becomes 16 and can be replaced at will by a new domicile of choice.

Double Jeopardy: A situation in which a person may be convicted twice for the same offence.

Drawee: The bank which has the drawer's checking account from which a check is to be paid.

Drawer: The person or organisation that has written a bill of exchange, such as a person who has written a cheque.

Dual Sovereignty Doctrine: A maxim of law which allows the double prosecution of a person by more than one state for the same crime, where both states have jurisdiction for the prosecution, and notwithstanding the double jeopardy rule.

Due Diligence: The formal process of investigating the background of a business, either prior to buying it, or as another party in a major contract. It is used to ensure that there are no hidden details that could affect the deal.

Duress: Forcing action or inaction against a person's will.

Duty: A legal obligation for a person to conduct himself to a certain standard failing which he could be liable for negligence if damages occur in the result or a levy charged by the Government, usually when things are bought, such as shares or buildings.

Duty of Care: The obligation of a person to exercise reasonable care in the conduct of an activity. Breach of a duty of care which causes damage or loss to another may give rise to an action in tort.

Ee

Easement: An interest in land owned by another that entitles its holder to a specific limited use or enjoyment *e.g.,* the right to cross the land, or to continue to have an unobstructed view over it.

Employment Contract: A contract between an employer and an employee. This differs from other contracts in that it is governed by employment legislation-which takes precedence over normal contract law.

Enabling Clause: A provision in new statute which empowers a particular public official to put it into effect, including making expenditures.

Enabling Legislation: Legislation which authorizes government ministers or bodies to create detailed rules to accomplish general principles set out in the legislation. For example, it may allow a minister to create rules or laws for a particular body, such as the police, to follow.

Encroachment: When a building or some portion of it, or a wall or fence, extends beyond the land of the owner and illegally intrudes upon that of an adjoining owner.

Encumbrance: Legal technical terminology for anything that affects or limits the title of a property, such as mortgages, leases, easements, liens, or restrictions.

Endorsement: The act of writing one's name on back of a note, bill, check or similar written instrument making the endorser a party to the instrument and liable, under certain conditions, for its payment.

Enduring Power: A power of attorney or guardianship which continues to have effect even if the donor ceases to be mentally competent.

Enforce: To make people obey (a law, the terms of an agreement, etc.).

Enforceable: A right or obligation is enforceable if the party obligated can be forced or ordered to comply through a legal process.

Enfranchisement of Tenancy: A method for acquiring the freehold or an extended lease of a leasehold house. A tenant has a statutory right of enfranchisement when he has a long lease (exceeding 21 years) and the house has been his *main residence for at least three years. The valuation of the freehold, or rent of an extended lease, is based on the value of the land without the buildings on it.

Engrossment: Preparing the final version of a legal document ready for it to be executed (made valid such as with a signature).

Equitable Mortgage: The type of mortgage where the purchaser owns the property which is security for the mortgage.

Equity: The value less liabilities of a property or business. Also means, Remedies under the law to determine fairness, right and justice.

Escalation Clause: A contract provision which permits the adjustment of contract prices by an amount or percent if certain specified contingencies occur, such as changes in the vendor's raw material or labor costs.

Escrow: The delivery of property conditionally to a third person (escrow holder), who holds it until the happening of an agreed upon event and then redelivers it to the owner according to the terms of the agreement.

Esquire: A mostly informal title associated with those who practice law.

Essoin: A valid excuse for not appearing in Court when summoned.

Estate: The interest which one may have in lands or other property. Also, the property of a deceased person.

Estate Freeze: A deferment of property transfer at the time of death to avoid, reduce or transfer tax liability.

Estoppel: A rule of law that a person cannot deny something they previously said, if someone else acted on what was said and their position was changed, possibly for the worse, as a result.

Et seq: 'And in the following pages'. It is sometimes written in books and documents. (This phrase is abbreviated from the Latin 'et sequeus'.)

Evaluation of Responses: The examination of responses after opening to determine the vendor's responsibility, responsiveness to requirements, and other characteristics of the solicitation relating to the award.

Eviction: The dispossession of a tenant of leased property by force or through the legal process.

Excess of Jurisdiction: Someone such as a judge acting without authority.

Exchange: The exchange of agreed, signed contracts. The transaction between the seller and the buyer is then legally binding, and completion (including the final transfer of money) usually takes place two to four weeks later.

Exchange of Contract: Swapping identical contracts. When land is sold, the person selling and the person buying both sign identical copies of the contract and exchange them. The contract is then binding on both of them.

Excise Duty: A type of tax levied on certain goods such as petrol. It is also levied on some activities such as gambling and on certain licenses for activities (such as driving a car on the public roads).

Exclusions: The things an insurance policy does not provide cover for. They will be listed in the insurance policy.

Exclusion Clauses: Clauses in a contract that are intended to exclude one party from liability if a stated circumstance happens. They are types of exemption clauses. The courts tend to interpret them strictly and, where possible, in favor of the party that did not write them. In customer dealings, exclusion clauses are governed by regulations that render most of them ineffective but note that these regulations do not cover you in business dealings.

Execution: A court order issued to enforce a judgment. Execution also refers to completion of a written instrument by signing, sealing, acknowledging, and delivering the instrument.

Exempt: To release or be free from some liability to which others are subject. Also, it can mean that property not available for seizure.

Exemption: The right given a debtor to retain authorized portions of his or her property, wages, or earnings from claims by creditors.

Exemption Clauses: Clauses in a contract that try to restrict the liability of the party that writes them. These are split into exclusion clauses that try to exclude liability completely for specified outcomes, and limitation clauses that try to set a maximum on the amount of damages the party may have to pay if there is a failure of some part of the contract. Exemption clauses are regulated very strictly in consumer dealings but these don't apply for those who deal in the course of their business.

Ex Gratia: Out of grace. A gift made without any obligation on the part of the giver or any return from the receiver.

Exhaustion of Rights: A free-trade principle which holds that, once goods are put on the market, owners of *intellectual property rights in those goods, who made the goods or allowed others to do so under their rights, may not use national intellectual property rights to prevent an import or export of the goods.

Exhibit: A document or thing shown to a witness when giving evidence, produced for inspection to the court or referred to in an affidavit.

Ex Parte: Is a Latin legal term meaning "from (by or for) one party. An ex parte decision is one decided by a judge without requiring all of the parties to the controversy to be present. In Australian, Canadian, U.K., Indian and U.S. legal doctrines, ex parte means a legal proceeding brought by one person in the absence of and without representation or notification of other parties. It is also used more loosely to refer to improper unilateral contacts with a court, arbitrator or represented party without notice to the other party or counsel for that party.

Expert Witness: A person who has been qualified as an expert and who then will be allowed (through answers to questions) to assist the jury in understanding complicated and technical subjects that are not generally within the jury's understanding. Medical doctors, accountants, and scientists commonly testify as expert witnesses.

Ex Post Facto: Ex post facto is a Latin term meaning "from a thing done afterward." Ex post facto often refers to a law that applies retroactively, thereby criminalizing conduct that was legal when originally performed.

Express Terms: The terms actually stated in the contract. These can be the written terms, or verbal ones agreed before or at the time the contract is made (see implied terms).

Expulsion: Permanent exclusion of a student from a school; compare: suspension.

Extended Sentence: A sentence longer than the maximum prescribed for a particular offence, which was formerly imposed on persistent offenders under certain circumstances.

Extinguishment: The cessation or cancellation of some right or interest.

Extortion: (Also called shakedown, out wresting, and exaction) is a criminal offence which occurs when a person unlawfully obtains money, property or services from a person(s), entity, or institution, through coercion.

Extradition: The surrender by one state to another of a person accused of committing an offence in the latter.

Extradition Treaty: A treaty under the terms of which a state agrees to deport a fugitive criminal (or suspect) to the state where the offence was committed or to the fugitive's state of nationality.

Extrinsic Evidence: Evidence of matters not referred to in a document offered in evidence to explain, vary, or contradict its meaning.

Ex Turpi Causa Non Oritur Action: [Latin: no action can be based on a disreputable cause] The principle that the courts may refuse to enforce a claim arising out of the claimant's own illegal or immoral conduct or transactions. Hence parties who have knowingly entered into an illegal contract may not be able to enforce it and a person injured by a fellow-criminal while they are jointly committing a serious crime may not be able to sue for damages for the injury.

Ex works: Available from the factory. When something is sold ex works the buyer can collect it from the place it was manufactured or from some other place agreed by the buyer and seller.

Ff

Facilitation: The uses of a neutral to help a group of people conduct productive discussions about complex or potentially controversial issues. The focus of the facilitator's role is to help people communicate effectively with each other.

Fact-Finding: A process in which a neutral, technical expert, or panel investigates and analyzes the facts and issues in a dispute and often issues a report to the parties and/or a court. The results of fact-finding are usually not binding, unless the parties have agreed otherwise, but may be admissible in court. Fact-finding is often a component of other ADR processes such as mediation and can take a variety of forms, including "neutral," "expert," or "joint fact-finding." In joint fact-finding, the parties designate representatives to work together to develop mutually acceptable responses to factual questions.

Failure of Consideration: Not delivering goods or services when promised in a contract.

False Imprisonment: Confinement of a person without legal permission.

False Pretence: Misleading someone by deliberately making a false statement.

False Representation: Lying in a statement to persuade someone to enter a contract.

Fictitious Trade Style: A term used in the transaction of business when the firm name does not clearly disclose the true name of the individual owner or partners.

Fiduciary: A person entrusted with the duty to act for the benefit of another person or who manages money or property for another.

Filing Claims: To preserve a creditor's rights and to receive its share of payment, it is often necessary to file a formal claim in a proper manner and within a time prescribed by law. Filing is generally required in bankruptcy matters, probate proceedings, assignments, receiverships and estates of minors and incompetents.

Fixed Assets: Any tangible property used in carrying on the operation of a business but will not be consumed or normally converted into cash (land, buildings, machinery, so forth).

Fixture: A permanently fixed piece of furniture or equipment incorporated into a property. Removing it would cause damage to buildings or land, and is therefore regarded as legally part of it.

Floating Charge: A form of security for a debt. Instead of naming a specific property, which can be taken by the creditor if the debtor defaults (as in a fixed charge like a mortgage), a class of goods or assets is named, such as the debtor's stock. This allows the debtor to trade in the assets freely, but if the debtor fails to make repayments then the floating charge becomes a fixed charge (known as crystallization) over all the stock at that time. The creditors can then take and sell it to recover the debt.

Fluctuation Clause: Contractual clause covering the procedure for handling price adjustments due to cost of living increases.

Forbearance: When one party to an agreement does not pursue rights under the agreement even though the other party has not kept to its terms. An example would be someone not suing to recover an overdue debt.

Force Majeure: A clause in contracts that excuses a party from not performing their contractual obligations due to unforeseen events beyond their control.

Forced Sale: A sale made under a court order and in the manner prescribed by law.

Foreclosure: A legal sale of mortgaged property by a creditor to obtain satisfaction of the mortgage out of the proceeds of the sale.

Foreign Corporation: A corporation created by and under the laws of a state other than the state in which it is doing business.

Forensic Procedure: Examination of the body of a person suspected of having committed an offence, or the taking of certain body samples.

Forfeiture: The loss of possession of a property because the tenancy conditions have not been met by the tenant.

Forgery: The offence of making a "false instrument" in order that it may be accepted as genuine, thereby causing harm to others.

Forward Contract: An agreement to buy or sell a specified thing at fixed price at some future date.

Forwarder: A forwarder may be an attorney, a collection agency, a credit bureau, a credit insurance company, or any other entity, which acts on behalf of the creditor as its agent, in the referral of claims for collection.

Forwarding Contract: A forwarding contract is the agreement entered into between the creditor and the receiver, specifying among other things the commission agreed upon between the receiver and the creditor as the receiver's compensation for effecting collection, in whole or in part, of a commercial claim.

Framework Agreement: An arrangement under which a contracting authority establishes with a provider of goods, works or services, the terms under which contracts subsequently can be entered into or called off (within the limits of the agreement) when particular needs arise. See also ('call-off contract').

Franchising: A franchise is a right granted to an individual or group to market a company's goods or services within a certain territory or location. Some examples of today's popular franchises are McDonald's, Subway, Domino's Pizza, and the UPS Store.

Franked Income: Formerly, income that a person or a company received on which*advance corporation tax had been paid. In the case of an individual the tax paid was imputed to the basic income-tax liability of the recipient. In the case of a company, it was imputed to its own liability to corporation tax.

Fraud: Intentionally dishonest act (or lack of action) done to deceive someone.

Fraudulent Conveyance: A transfer of property with the intention to defraud a creditor or avoid payment of a debt.

Fraudulent Preference: Someone who is insolvent paying one of their creditors while knowing there is not enough money to pay the others.

Fraudulent Trading: Running a business with the intention of defrauding its creditors or other people.

Free Demand Letter: A pre-collection letter sent by a collection agency to a debtor requesting that payment be made to a creditor by a given date.

Freehold: Outright ownership of a property. This type of tenure contrasts with leasehold where the leaseholder has the rights to occupy a property for a specified period of time.

Freedom of Association: The right to belong, or not belong, to an industrial association (trade union).

Freedom of Contract: That men and woman have the liberty of contracting as they see fit with the expectation that those contracts will be judicially enforced if necessary, subject only to public policy.

Freedom of Information: The right of any person to have access to documents held by government agencies, except those exempted by legislation.

Free of Encumbrances: No one else having any rights over something. When property is owned by someone and nobody else has any rights over it, it is owned free of encumbrances.

Frustration of Contract: Legal termination of a contract due to unforeseen circumstances that: 1. prevent achievement of its objectives, 2. render its performance illegal, or 3. make it practically impossible to execute. It could be caused by reasons such as an accident, change in law, fire, sickness of one of the parties, third-party interference. Frustration of a contract excuses non-performance and automatically discharges the contract except where the terms of contract override this implied legal provision. However, frustration is not acceptable as an excuse where the circumstance was foreseeable, and is not applicable to certain types of contracts such as insurance policies.

Futures Contract: A binding contract to buy or sell something on a date in the future at a fixed price.

Gg

Gag Order: A judge's order prohibiting the attorneys and the parties to a pending lawsuit of criminal prosecution from talking to the media of the public about the case.

Garnishee: A person or entity having possession of money or property belonging to a defendant, who is served with a writ of attachment or execution.

Garnishment: The legal process by which property due to a debtor and in the hands of a third person is attached.

Gift: A transfer of property with nothing given in return.

Good Faith: Honesty. An act carried out in good faith is one carried out honestly. Good faith is implied by law into certain contracts, such as those relating to commercial agency.

Goodwill: The advantage arising from the reputation and trade connections of a business, in particular the likelihood that existing customers will continue to patronize it. Goodwill is a substantial item to be taken into account on the sale of a business; it may need to be protected by prohibiting the vendor from setting up in the same business for a stated period in competition with the business he has sold.

Going Concern: A term for a company that has the resources needed in order to continue to operate indefinitely. If a company is not a going concern, it means the company has gone bankrupt.

Golden Handshake: A payment, usually very large, made to a director or other senior executive who is forced to retire before the expiry of an employment contract (*e.g.*, because of a takeover or merger) as compensation for loss of office. It is made when a contract does not allow payment in lieu of notice.

Golden Hello: A lump-sum payment to entice an employee of senior level to join a new employer. Whether or not the payment is tax-free depends on the nature of the payment.

Grand-Father Clause: A provisions in law or a contract which exempts persons already engaging in the activity which the law or contract prohibits, from adverse results from the subsequent law or contract.

Guarantee: A secondary agreement by which one person promises to honor the debt of another if that debtor fails to pay. Banks and other creditors often call on directors of small companies to give their personal guarantees for company debts. A guarantee must be in writing. The guarantor can only be sued if the actual debtor can't pay, in contrast to indemnity.

Guarantee Company: A company whose members only have to pay the amount they have agreed to contribute, if the company has to be wound up. They do not have to pay in extra money if there is not enough to pay all the company's debts.

Guardian: A person who has the right and duty to protect another person, his or her property and rights. A plenary guardian has all the powers of a parent.

Guarantor: A person who undertakes to guaranty something or act as surety.

Guilty: A court's verdict that the person charged with a crime committed it.

Hh

Habeas Corpus: Latin: a court petition which orders that a person being detained be produced before a judge for a hearing to decide whether the detention is lawful.

Habitable: Suitable and fit for a person to live in and free of any faults that might endanger the health and safety of occupants.

Habitual Offender: A person who is convicted and sentenced for crimes over a period of time and even after serving sentences of incarceration, demonstrates a propensity towards future criminal conduct.

Hearing: Legal proceedings in which arguments of the interested parties are heard in court.

Hearsay Evidence: Evidence of a fact not personally seen or heard by a witness, but proved by him or her to have been said by another. Hearsay evidence is normally not admissible in court proceedings, but there are exceptions to this rule.

Hired Gun: An expert with a bias or who adapts his or her expert evidence to the requirements of the party that calls him/her as a witness.

Hire Purchase: Where goods are sold with installment payments required from the purchaser. No rights of ownership lie with the purchaser until the last payment due has been made

Hissing: A common law right given to the audiences of public performances to openly express their opinion of the performance.

Holding Company: A company which controls another company, usually by owning more than half of its shares.

Holdover Tenancy: A tenancy that arises when someone remains in possession of a property after the expiration of the previous tenancy and is recognized by the landlord by accepting rent.

Holograph Will: A will written entirely in the testator's handwriting and not witnessed.

Home-Country Rule: A form of international agreement in which a host country allows a foreign national to continue to fall under the exclusive jurisdiction of his country of origin even as regards acts or commerce in the host country.

Homestead: To record a homestead, exempts such a home from legal execution or forced sale in satisfaction of certain debts, except any excess over the exempt value. Individual state laws apply.

Hostile Witness: A witness who: refuses to testify in support of the people who called them; or testifies in a way which differs from their previous statement.

House of Lords: The highest court in the UK.

Housing Associations: Organizations run to provide housing for people. They are not intended to make a profit.

Hung Jury: A jury whose members cannot reconcile their differences of opinion and thus cannot reach a verdict.

Hypothecation: A person giving a bank authority to sell goods which have been pledged to the bank as security for a loan.

Ii

Id est (ie): That is. Is followed by a definition or list of items or options that relate to a preceding statement or condition. Differs from exempli gratia (eg)—for example—that gives some, but not all, examples of the items or options.

Immovable: Land and fixtures thereto, civil law term.

Immunity: An exemption that a person enjoys from the normal operation of the law such as a legal duty or liability, either criminal or civil.

Impaired: A deterioration of an individual's judgment and decrease in his or her's physical ability. Used primarily in criminal law; driving under the influence of alcohol or disability law in regards to a person's physical or mental impairment.

Impanel: Also, "empanel"; the official call to duty of a jury, usually as called by the clerk of the court in which the jury is to act, and just before the jurors are sworn in.

Implied Contract: An agreement which is found to exist based on the circumstances when deny a contract would be unfair and/or result in unjust enrichment to one of the parties.

Implied Terms: Are terms and clauses that are implied in a contract by law or custom and practice without actually being mentioned by any party. Terms implied by custom and practice can always be overridden by express terms, but some terms implied by law cannot be overridden, particularly those relating to consumers (see exemption clauses).

Implied Trust: A trust that is imposed by law onto certain situations either by presuming an intention of the participants to create a trust, or simply because of the facts at hand.

Implied Undertaking Rule: A party to whom documents are produced within litigation will not use them for collateral or ulterior purposes.

Imputation of Payments: A civil law term: a system that allocates monies received from a debtor who has more than one debt and who has not, with the payment, specified to the creditor to which debt the monies are applied.

Inchmaree Clause: A standard clause in maritime insurance contracts covering risk of events not directly linked to perils at sea such as, but not necessarily limited to, loading accidents.

Inchoate: A legal right or entitlement that is in progress and is neither ripe, vested nor perfected.

Inchoate Offence: Acts which are criminal even though they precede harmful conduct.

Income Tax: A mandatory payment imposed on residents of a pro-rated portion of their income as a contribution towards the costs of government services.

Incorporate: Inclusion in, or adoption of, some term or condition as part of the contract. It differs from its company law definition where it refers to the legal act of creating a company.

Indict: Using legal means, to officially accuse someone of committing an offence.

Indemnify: A promise by a third party to pay a debt owed, or repay a loss caused, by another party. Unlike a guarantee, the person owed can get the money direct from the indemnifier without having to chase the debtor first. Insurance contracts are contracts of indemnity: the insurance company pays first, and then tries to recover the loss from whoever caused it.

Indemnity: An agreement to insure or reimburse another in case of damage or failure to fulfill an obligation.

Indenture: A deed or other document to which two or more parties are bound.

Indictable Offence: A crime (offense) for which a grand jury rules that there is enough evidence to charge defendant with a felony (a crime punishable by death or a term in the state penitentiary). These crimes include murder, manslaughter, rape, kidnaping, grand theft, robbery, burglary, arson, conspiracy, fraud, and other major crimes, as well as attempts to commit them.

Indictment: A document setting out the details of the offence a defendant is accused of.

Inferior court: Any of the courts that are subordinate to superior courts, having a jurisdiction limited to a particular geographical area, size of claim, or type of case. Their decisions are normally subject to appeal to a superior court, and the exercise of their jurisdiction may be subject to control by a superior court.

Inherent Jurisdiction: The residual, automatic and ex-officio authority of a court of law to regulate proceedings before it including punishing contempt.

Inhibition: A legal procedure to prevent a debtor from compromising property upon which a creditor holds a charge.

Injunction: A remedy sometimes awarded by the court that stops some action being taken. It can be used to stop another party doing something against the terms of the contract. Injunctions are at the court's discretion and a judge may refuse to give one and award damages instead.

In Lieu: In place of.

Insolvency: The situation where a person or business cannot pay its debts as they fall due (see bankruptcy, liquidation and receivership).

Intangible Property: Property which does not physically exist, such as a right or a patent.

Inter Alia: Among other things. This is often used in contracts to indicate that what is being specifically referred to is part of a larger group without having to name all the elements.

Interim Payment: A payment made while waiting for other payments, or the size of other payments, to be decided

Interim Payment Certificates: A payment certificate issued under the Clause "Contract Price and Payment", other than the Final Payment Certificate.

Interim relief: Preliminary relief, such as an injunction, granted by the court to preserve the status quo pending trial.

Interlocutory: Provisional; temporary; not final—refers to orders and decrees of a court.

Interpleader: Action by which one having possession of an article or fund claimed by two parties may compel them to litigate the title between themselves, instead of with him/her.

Interpreter: A person sworn at a judicial proceeding to translate oral or written language.

Interpretation Clause: To assist in the interpretation of the intentions of the parties, many standard forms include a clause defining particular words and phrases used in the contract.

Interrogatories: A series of formal written questions used in the examination of a party or a witness prior to trial.

Intervening Cause: An event that interrupts the chain of causation by providing an independent cause of the final result, possibly relieving the original actors of liability.

Intestate: A person who dies without a will.

Invitation to Tender: An invitation to contractors, suppliers or service providers to bid for the provision of works, goods or services.

Invitation to Treat: An invitation to another person to make an offer to contract.

Invitee: A person, such as a customer, who is present in a place either by the express or the implied invitation of the occupier. This normally means that the occupier has to exercise reasonable care to protect the safety of the invited person.

Issued Share Capital: Share capital which has been allocated to shareholders who have subscribed for (asked for) shares.

Jj

Jay Walking: Violation of traffic regulations, particularly when crossing a street or road other than at an intersection, or failure to used designated pedestrian crosswalks or to obey pedestrian traffic signals.

Joint and Several Liabilities: Where parties act together in a contract as partners they have joint and several liabilities. In addition to all the partners being responsible together, each partner is also liable individually for the entire contract—so a creditor could recover a whole debt from any one of them individually, leaving that person to recover their shares from the rest of the partners.

Joint Liability: It is a legal obligation between two or more persons against claims or damages incurred by them jointly for which they are equally and jointly responsible. In such a case no party can be sued individually.

Joint Tenancy: A joint holding of property by two or more persons with agreement that upon the death of one, the full title to the estate shall remain with the survivor.

Joint Trial: Two or more actions involving a common question of law or fact may be joined by court order for trial—the actions are not merged but remain separate and distinct and may result in one or more verdicts and judgments.

Joint Venture: An agreement between two or more independent businesses in a business enterprise, in which they will share the costs, management, profits or benefits arising from the venture. The exact shares and responsibilities will be set out in a Joint Venture Agreement.

Judgment: A formal court decree granting or denying a plaintiff's claim.

Judgment: A decision given by a court of law.

Judgment debt: The amount awarded to be paid under a court order.

Judgment Proof: A judgment debtor from whom collection cannot be made because the person has no assets or has concealed or removed property subject to execution.

Judgment Roll: A record of the judgment with the supporting papers.

Judicial Review: Review by a court of an administrative act on the basis of fault in the decision-making process. Compare: review on the merits.

Judicial Lien: A lien obtained by judgment, levy or other legal proceeding.

Judicial Notice: The court's authority to accept matters of common knowledge or indisputable fact without anyone having to present evidence on the point.

Judicial Precedent: Refers to a previous judicial decision or proceeding that is available and may be relied upon in case any dispute arises.

Jurisdiction: A jurisdiction clause sets out the country or state whose laws will govern the contract and where any legal action must take place.

Juror: One of the people who are acting as a jury.

Jury: A group of people (usually 12) who review all the evidence in a court case and then come to a verdict.

Justice: A state of affairs in which conduct or action is both fair and right, given the circumstances.

Justice of the Peace: A judicial officer with a limited role, usually in criminal law, to perform minor judicial tasks such as authorizing search warrants and approving criminal charges.

Justiciability: Refers to the types of matters that the federal courts can adjudicate. If a case is "nonjusticiable." a federal court cannot hear it. To be justiciable, the court must not be offering an advisory opinion, the plaintiff must have standing, and the issues must be ripe but neither moot nor violative of the political question doctrine.

A necessary prerequisite of a matter put to a court of law for resolution; that an actual and substantial controversy be at hand.

Justification: claiming that a defamatory statement is true. In a defamation case a defendant may admit that the claimant ('plaintiff' before April 1999)'s allegations are true but plead that the statement which defamed was true.

Justifying Bail: Proving to the court that the person giving the surety has the assets to pay the bail.

Juvenile Offender: A person aged between 10 and 17 who have committed a criminal offence.

Kk

Kangaroo Court: A judicial proceeding or trial which has a predetermined outcome or where the basic legal rights of a party are jumped over.

Keeper: A custodian installed in a place of business by a levying officer under an execution or attachment, for the purpose of realizing payment from the defendant (debtor) either voluntarily or by a legal (forced) sale of the assets.

Key-Man Insurance: Life insurance to protect a business upon the death of a key individual

Knock and Announce Rule: A standard requirement of police officers executing a search warrant that they first knock on the main entry door and announce the purpose of their attendance.

Knock and Talk: An investigation technique involving a law enforcement officer attending at the door of certain premises to speak with the occupants, or asking for consent to search the premises.

Knock out Agreement: An agreement by dealers not to bid against each other at an auction. Such an agreement is illegal.

Know-how: The expertise in an organization which may be protected by a patent.

Knowing Receipt: If a stranger receives trust property knowing it to be in breach of trust, he will be liable to account to the beneficiaries for that property or for the proceeds of it.

Knowingly: Acting voluntarily and intentionally and not because of mistake or accident.

Knowingly Concerned: Consciously and deliberately involved in committing an offence.

Known Loss Doctrine: A principle of insurance law which prevents an insured from coverage if the insured knew the loss was probable at the time of the insurance contract.

Ll

Laches: Doctrine of Laches limits the legal claim of a person, by virtue of any undue delay on his part in enforcing his legal right. For example, a person failed to initiate any action to recover his property, after knowing that it was used by another person. He lose his right to claim the property when he initiate the process to recover his property after consumption or transformation of the property the possessor.

Landlord: The owner of property that is leased or rented to others.

Latent Defect: A hidden flaw that cannot be readily ascertained from mere observation.

Law List: A directory of attorneys.

Law Report: A law report is a written record of a court case. A single case can be reported in more than one series of law reports.

Lawsuit: A claim made in a court of law.

Lay-Off: A temporary discharge of an employee.

Lease: A contract by which an owner of property conveys exclusive possession and use of it for a specified rent and for a specified period—after which the property reverts to the owner.

Lease Contract: An agreement under which equipment or facilities can be obtained on a rental payment basis for a given period of time.

Legal Composition: Identification and description of the lawful ownership or title to a business.

Legal duty: The responsibility to others to act according to the law.

Legal Professional Privilege: A shield against disclosure of communications between a solicitor and his/her client.

Legal Tender: Currency that may be lawfully tendered in payment of a debt, such as paper money, Federal Reserve notes, or coins.

Legally Binding: Able to be enforced by law.

Legislation: Written and approved laws.

Letter of Acceptance: A letter that creates an immediate binding contractual relationship between the Council and the successful tenderer prior to entering into a formal contract.

Letters of Administration: The document by which a person is empowered to manage the estate of a deceased who left no valid will.

Letter of Credence: A formal document by which the head of an accredited state presents its newly appointed diplomatic agent to the head of state of the host country.

Letter of Credit: A letter addressed by a banker to a correspondent bank guaranteeing payment, when evidenced by documents confirming shipment of goods. This can be an irrevocable or revocable letter of credit.

Letter of Demand: A notice from a creditor that legal action will be taken if a debt is not paid.

Letter of Intent: A letter informing a successful tenderer that it is the Council's intention to enter into a contract with them in the future but creates no liability in regard to that future contract.

Lessee: A person to whom property is leased.

Lessor: A person who leases property to another.

Levy: An action by a court officer to satisfy an execution or attachment by the seizure and holding or sale of property.

Liability: A person or business deemed liable is subject to a legal obligation. A person/business who commits a wrong or breaks a contract or trust is said to be liable or responsible for it.

Liabilities: Obligations or debts owed by a business to its creditors.

Libel: Written or printed words (or pictures) that degrade or defame a person.

Lien: A legal claim or hold which one person has upon the property of another as security for the payment of a debt or performance of an obligation.

Limited Liability: Usually refers to limited companies where the owners' liability to pay the debts of the company is limited to the value of their shares. It can also apply to contracts where a valid limitation clause has been included in the terms.

Limited Partnership: A business organization with one or more general partners, who manage the business and assume legal debts and obligations, and one or more limited partners, who are liable only to the extent of their investments. Limited partners also enjoy rights to the partnership's cash flow, but are not liable for company obligations.

Liquidated Account: An account that is certain, fixed and settled as to amount by the act and agreement of the parties or through law.

Liquidation: Is the process by which a company (or part of a company) is brought to an end, and the assets and property of the company redistributed. Liquidation is also sometimes referred to as winding-up or dissolution, although dissolution technically refers to the last stage of liquidation.

Liquidator: A person assigned to supervise the liquidation of a business concern and whose legal authorization, rights, and duties differ according to whether the liquidation is compulsory or voluntary.

Litigation: An action brought in court to enforce a particular right. The act or process of bringing a lawsuit in and of itself; a judicial contest; any dispute. When a person begins a civil lawsuit, the person enters into a process called litigation.

Loan Capital: Money raised by a company issuing *debentures. The aggregate amount borrowed by the company with each issue is sometimes referred to as stock.

Loan creditor: A person or organisation which has lent money to an organization.

Lock-out Agreement: A contract between a potential purchaser and the vendor of a property in which the vendor agrees that for a fixed period, such as two weeks, he will take the house off the market and not accept any other offers. Meanwhile the purchaser moves towards a quick *exchange of contracts, with the aim of securing the sale within that period. If the vendor breaches the agreement by accepting another offer, he can be sued for *breach of contract. Many vendors will not accept such agreements and some lawyers have argued they are unenforceable.

Long Form Order: An order prepared by counsel for signature of the court (usually based on a memorandum decision).

Loss of Amenity: Loss or reduction of a claimant's mental or physical capacity to do the things he used to do, suffered as a result of personal injuries. In actions for personal injuries the claimant may recover damages for loss of the amenities of life, in addition to his financial losses and an award for pain and suffering. Thus loss of the ability to play games or a musical instrument, if these were the claimant's hobbies, will be taken into account in fixing damages. The assessment is based on an objective view of the value of the loss of these amenities to the claimant.

Loss of Use: The inability to use an automobile, premise or some equipment due to damage to the vehicle, premises or articles caused by the negligence or other wrongdoing of another.

Lost Productivity: Productivity is "lost" on the project when the contractor's actual amount of labor or equipment hours is greater than the hours planned in its bid. Another way of encountering "lost" productivity is when the contractor accomplishes less work than planned using the same amount of labor or equipment resources within the same planned time frame. In either case, the contractor is expending more labor or equipment resources per unit for work actually accomplished. The terms "lost" productivity, disruption, and inefficiency are often used interchangeably, without distinction.

Lump-sum Award: The form in which damages are given by a court. The award covers both past losses (up to the time of judgment) and losses likely to be suffered in the future. The general rule is that only one award of damages may be made, unless the wrong is a continuing one (such as continuing trespass or nuisance). However, *interim payments can be ordered pending the final estimation of damages, and in actions for personal injuries in which the claimant may develop some serious disease or suffer some serious deterioration in his condition,*provisional damages may be given. This enables the claimant to comeback for further damages at a future date if the disease or deterioration occurs. Settlements of personal injury cases out of court can include periodic payments as well as a lump sum as part of a structured settlement.

Mm

Magistrate: A Justice of the Peace who presides over (is in charge of) minor cases heard in the magistrates 'court'.

Mailbox Rule: A contract law exception that makes a mailed acceptance of an offer valid as of posting.

Mala fides: Bad faith, opposite of bona fide.

Malfeasance: An unlawful act.

Malicious Prosecution: An intentional tort which redresses losses flowing from an unjustified prosecution.

Mandate Rule: An inferior court has no power or authority to deviate from the mandate issued by an appellate court.

Marginal Business: A sale made to a credit risk from whom payment may be delayed because the business may not have sufficient operating capital.

Marital Property: Property acquired by either of two spouses while they are married together.

Marshal: An officer of the court whose duties correspond to those of a Sheriff in relation to civil process.

Master: Legal officer of the Supreme Court empowered to perform auxiliary judicial duties.

Material form: Any form of storage from which a copyright work can be reproduced.

Mayhem: Violently depriving another person of a body part to render less effective that person's defence of self.

Means Test: Assessment of a person's income and assets to see if they qualify for financial assistance.

Mediation: Form of dispute resolution where an impartial third party helps communication and negotiations between the parties, but does not decide the dispute.

Memorandum and Articles of Association: The memorandum gives details of a company's name, objects (purposes) and share capital. It also sets out the limits of the shareholders' liability if the company has to be wound up. The articles set out the members' rights and the directors' powers.

Memorandum Decision: A written opinion or decision of a court on a litigated question, giving the court's conclusion on factual and legal issues (this may constitute the order of the court if so stated.

Memorandum of Understanding (MOU): A formalized written document between two or more parties that defines the interests, expectations and obligations of each party.

Memorandum Opinion: Memorandum in writing, which is a very brief statement of the reasons for a decision, without detailed explanation.

Mercantile Law: The branch of the law dealing with commerce.

Merchantable Quality: The assumption in the law that goods sold by a business will be fit for their purpose.

Mini Trial: Two-step process to facilitate settlement in which (*a*) the parties attorneys present a summary of the evidence and arguments they expect to offer at trial to a neutral in the presence of individuals with decision-making authority for each party, and (*b*) the individuals with decision-making authority meet with or without the neutral to discuss settlement of the case.

Minor: A person who is under age or has not reached legal maturity as prescribed by a state.

Minutes of Meeting: The official written record of a meeting. Minutes may be kept by any individual in attendance at a meeting and are usually distributed to all members of the unit represented at the meeting.

Miscarriage of Justice: The court system failing to give justice to someone.

Misrepresentation: Where one party to a contract makes a false statement of fact to the other which that other person relies on. Where there has been a misrepresentation then the party who was misled can get damages for their loss.

Mistrial: A trial that is vitiated by some fundamental defect.

Mitigation: Circumstances which go towards reducing the damages or punishment which the court may order against a defendant or prisoner.

Mixed Action: A form of court action combining a claim relating to real property with a claim for damages.

Mixed Fund: A fund of money derived from the sale of both real and personal property.

Mixed Property: Property that has some of the attributes of both real and personal property.

Moiety: A portion of something, typically half.

Monopoly: Monopoly describes being the only one in a given market selling a specific product, or having exclusive control over a certain thing or a board game where the aim is to buy properties on the board and then build hotels on those properties.

Moot: A mock trial, often held in university law schools and at the Inns of Court, for students as practice for future advocacy. A hypothetical case is presented to students for preparation and then argued before the judge(s) at the moot. This practice originates in the formal moots held in the medieval Inns of Court, which were considered an essential part of legal education.

Moral Law: The body of laws to which individuals feel themselves subject, often through their religious beliefs.

Moratorium: An agreement not to take action to recover a debt for an agreed period of time.

Mortgage: A conditional conveyance of property as security for the payment of a debt or the performance of a duty, that becomes void upon payment or performance according to the stipulated terms; usually applicable to personal or real property.

Mortgage Action: A court action brought by a mortgagee for possession of the mortgaged property or payment of all money due to him, when the mortgagor has failed to pay the amounts due under the mortgage.

Mortgagee: A person that takes or receives a mortgage.

Mortgagor: The party who makes a mortgage.

Motion: An application, either written or oral, addressed to the court requesting a ruling on a matter of law or equity.

Movant: The party who initiates the motion.

Multiple Admissibility: Multiple admissibility is a principle of evidence law. According to multiple admissibility when evidence is admissible for one purpose it should not be rejected solely because it is inadmissible for some other purpose.

Multiple Awards: Contracts awarded to more than one supplier for comparable supplies and services. Awards are made for the same generic types of items at various prices.

Muniments: Documents that prove a person's title to land. They include the relevant title deeds, certificates of official search, and other documents tracing ownership of the land through to the present owner.

Mutual Wills: Wills conferring reciprocal benefits, made by two or more persons who have agreed that the wills are not to be revoked. The court will enforce the agreement by declaring that the survivor holds the relevant property on*constructive trust to give effect to the mutual will.

Nn

Naked Trust: A trust which holds property for a person until they ask the trustee to return it.

Naturalization: Giving a citizen of one country citizenship of another.

Natural Rights: Also called inalienable rights, are considered to be self-evident and universal. They are not contingent upon the laws, customs, or beliefs of any particular culture or government.

Necessities of Life: Essentials commonly required by all persons to maintain life (whatever their employment or status), *e.g.*, food, clothing, shelter, medical care, light and heat, etc.

Negligence: The failure by a reasonable person to use sufficient care, diligence and skill which he required to use for the protection of others from injury or damage.

Negotiable (Instrument): An instrument obligating the payment of money which is transferable from one person to another by endorsement and delivery or by delivery only.

Negotiated Contract: Contract awarded on the basis of a direct agreement with a contractor, without going through the competitive bidding process.

Negotiation (in International Law): A diplomatic procedure by which representatives of states, either by direct personal contact or through correspondence, engage in discussing matters of mutual concern and attempt to resolve disputes that have arisen in relations between themselves.

Negotiation of a Bill: The transfer of a *bill of exchange from one person to another so that the transferee becomes the holder. A bill payable to bearer is negotiated by delivery; a bill payable to order is negotiated by the *endorsement of the holder completed by delivery. The issue of a bill to the payee is not a negotiation.

Nemodat Quod Non Habet: No one can give what they do not have. The principle that a seller cannot pass on a better right to the property than they actually have. So, if goods are stolen, the buyer does not get ownership even if there was no indication that they were stolen.

Net: The full amount the customer is expected to pay. The amount left after necessary deductions are taken out.

Net Worth: The total assets of a business less the total liabilities.

Neutral Citation: A legal citation unique to cases issued from a particular court with numbering assigned sequentially, and designed for electronic database and Internet cataloging retrieval.

No Asset Case: An insolvent estate with no dividend available or possible for creditors.

Non-Contingent Suit Fee: Money sent to the attorney which is kept for filing a lawsuit.

Non compos Mentis: Not of sound mind. A person who is not of sound mind will not have full capacity to enter into a contract.

Non-Dischargeable Debt: Certain debts are not included in the debtor's discharge. Some are automatically excluded. Others to be excluded require action by the creditor.

Non est Factum: Not my act. This is a denial by a person that they were actually involved in some action or dealings. In a contract, it can occur if a party denies that they signed the contract-that someone else forged their signature.

Non-executive Director: A director who does not work directly for a company but advises the other directors. Non-executive directors have the full powers and authority of any other director and can bind the company to any contract.

Non Provable Debt: A debt that cannot be claimed in the course of bankruptcy proceedings. Examples are statute-barred debts and debts that cannot be fixed or estimated.

Nonsuit: 1. The withdrawal by a judge of a case from a jury with a verdict being entered in favor of the accused. 2. Formerly, a claimant's withdrawal from a civil court action.

Nominated Sub-contractor: Means any merchant tradesman specialist or other person firm or company nominated in accordance with the Contract to be employed by the Contractor for the execution of work or supply of goods materials or services for which a Prime Cost has been inserted in the Contract or ordered by the Engineer to be employed by the Contractor to execute work or supply goods materials or services under a Provisional Sum.

Notary (Notary Public): A legal practitioner, usually a solicitor, who attests or certifies deeds and other documents and notes or *protests dishonored bills of exchange.

Note: Terms highlighted in bold within the current definitions (*e.g.*, wound up).

Not Guilty: 1. A denial of the charges by an accused person in court. If there is more than one charge, the accused may plead guilty to some and not guilty to others. 2. A verdict finding that an accused person has not committed the offence with which he was charged. However, he may, at the same time, be found guilty of other offences.

Notices: This is a clause that provides that all notices should be in writing and that all parties must contact each other if there is a change in address. Since all changes to the contract terms must be in writing, written correspondence and contact information is critical.

Notice of Entry: A notice with an affidavit of service stating that the attached copy of an entered order or judgment has been served by a party on another party.

Notice of Motion: A formal notice to participants in litigation of an intent to seek specific relief in an action.

Notice of Petition: Written notice of a petitioner that a hearing will be held in a court to determine the relief requested in an annexed petition.

Notice of Protest: A formal statement that a certain bill of exchange, check or promissory note was presented for payment or acceptance, and that such payment or acceptance was refused.

Notice to Quit: A notification or communication to a tenant to leave specified premises usually for a breach of terms of the lease.

Notional Earnings: Weekly wages currently earned or that the worker is considered capable of earning.

Notional: Relating to, expressing, or consisting of notions or ideas or not evident in reality or hypothetical or imaginary.

Novation Contract: The substitution of a new contract for an old one. The new agreement extinguishes the rights and obligations that were in effect under the old agreement.

Null: Having no legal or binding force; invalid: "the interim government was declared null and void".

Nulla Bona: Return of writ of execution by the sheriff after a search has been made and no assets found.

Nunc pro tunc: (Now for then) presently considered as if occurring at an earlier date; effective retroactively.

Oo

Oath: A pledge that statements made are true which is made with one's hand on the Bible. Witnesses in court are required to take an oath or make an affirmation before giving evidence.

Obiter Dictum: Latin: An observation by a judge on a matter not specifically before the court or not necessary in determining the issue before the court.

Objection in Point of Law: A form of pleading by a defendant in his defence that raises an issue of law. When such an objection is raised the court may order the issue to be tried as a *preliminary point of law.

Objection to Indictment: A procedure in which the accused in a *trial on indictment attempts to prove some objection to the indictment on legal grounds (*e.g.*, that it contravenes, or fails to comply with, an enactment). The objection is raised by application to quash the indictment.

Objects of a Power: Persons in whose favor a power of appointment may be exercised, *i.e.*, potential appointees.

Obligations: A legal requirement established by law, contract or as a result of unlawful harm caused to the person or property of another.

Obligee: The person who is to receive the benefit of someone else's obligation.

Obligor: A person who is contractually or legally, committed or obliged, to providing something to another person (the obligee).

Obliteration: The deletion of words in a will. Obliteration is valid only if the words deleted are indecipherable or if the alteration is properly signed and witnessed.

Objection: Protesting something and referring the question of its propriety or legality to the court.

Obscenity: A publication which is illegal because it is morally corruptive.

Obscurities: Things which are not clear.

Obstructing Justice: An act which tends to impede or thwart the administration of justice.

Occupancy: Holding, possessing, or occupying premises.

Occupant: Someone who occupies a particular place.

Occupiers' Liability: Liability of a person who controls land or building(s) in regards to damages caused to others who enters thereon.

Offer: An offer to contract must be made with the intention to create, if accepted, a legal relationship. It must be capable of being accepted (not containing any impossible conditions), must also be complete (not requiring more information to define the offer) and not merely advertising.

Offence: A wrong prohibited by the criminal law.

Offender: A person who commits an offence.

Official Referee: For practical purposes, one of the judges who used to hear building contract cases in the UK High Court.

Official referee's Schedule: More commonly known as a Scott Schedule. A form of pleading commonly used in the official referee's court, where the contentions of the parties appear in tabular form.

Official Solicitor: An officer of the Supreme Court who, when directed by the court, acts as *1itigation friend (next friend) or children's guardian for those under a disability who have no one else to act for them; he may also be called upon to intervene and protect the interests of children. He can be appointed *judicial trustee in proceedings relating to disputed trusts.

Omissions: Items of original contract work required not to be carried out by the employer or the architect on the employer's behalf.

Onus of Proof: Burden of proof .

Opening Statement: The first address of counsel prior to offering of evidence.

Operative: Synonym for workman.

Option: The exercise of the power of choice; also, a privilege which may give one the exclusive right to buy or sell property at a given price within a specified time.

Oral Proof: Evidence given by word of mouth; the oral testimony of a witness.

Order: An oral or written direction of a court or judge.

Out-of-Court Settlement: An agreement between two litigants to settle a matter privately before the Court has rendered its decision.

Overriding Error: A standard of appellate review, an error that must have altered the result or may well have altered the result.

Own Motion: Decision by a body to take action, *e.g.*, to start an investigation, without a complaint having been made.

Pp

Paid Direct: Payment made straight to the actual payee, without sending it through an intermediary or a third party.

Paralegal: A person who is not a lawyer or is not acting in that capacity but who provides a limited number of legal services.

Parent Company: Where one company owns more than 50 per cent of the voting rights of another company it is the parent of that company which in turn becomes its subsidiary. It can also occur where the parent has less than 50 per cent but can control the board of directors of the subsidiary—that is, it has the power to appoint and remove directors without referring to other shareholders.

Parent Company Guarantee: A parent company guarantee binds the guarantor (the 'parent company') to fulfill and complete a subsidiary company's obligations and liabilities in the event of failure by that subsidiary to fulfill and complete its obligations and liabilities under a contract.

Paripassu: Equal and even. This relates to shares to denote that newly issued shares have the same rights and restrictions as those of the same class already existing.

Parole: A conditional release from incarceration during which a prisoner promises to heed certain conditions (usually set by a parole board) and submits to the supervision of a parole officer.

Parole Evidence: Refers to verbal expressions or words. Verbal evidence, such as the testimony of a witness at trial.

Parole Evidence Rule: The meaning of a contract cannot be changed by reference to statements made by the parties to the contract before the contract was formed.

Particulars: A written, detailed statement of the items of a plaintiff's demand, or the defendant's setoff in a lawsuit.

Particulars of Claim: A document which sets out the details of the allegations made in a legal dispute.

Partition: The division into parts of property held jointly, or the sale of such property by a court with division of the proceeds.

Partnering: Establishing a long term win-win relationship based on mutual trust and teamwork, and on sharing of both risks and rewards. Partnering arrangement can be between labor and management, subordinates and the executive, suppliers, customers. The objective is to focus on what each party does best, by sharing financial and other resources, and establishing specific roles for each participant.

Partnership: An association of two or more persons (or entities) to carry on as co-owners of a business and sharing in its profits or losses (not necessarily equally).

Party Wall: It is referred to the wall created on the boundary of the two properties and which serves as a common structure between the two premises owned by different parties. The wall may be partly on each property or fully on one's property but is still a common structure. It is the duty of party of each property to maintain the wall.

Passage of Risk: Stage in a transaction at which the risk of loss and damage passes on from the seller to the buyer. Different trading terms have different points where passage of risk occurs. In FOB terms, for example, it occurs when the shipment reaches its destination; in CIF terms it occurs when the shipment is delivered to the carrier.

Past-Due: Payment delayed beyond an agreed upon settlement date.

Patent: A form of protection that provides a person or legal entity with exclusive rights for making, using or selling a concept or invention and excludes others from doing the same for the duration of the patent.

Patent Defect: Defect in material and/or workmanship that may cause failure or malfunction of an item, and is discoverable upon its inspection.

Payment: The partial or complete discharge of an obligation by its settlement in the form of the transfer of funds, assets, or services equal to the monetary value of part or all of the debtor's obligation.

Pecuniary: Involving money. So: pecuniary loss—loss of an amount of money; pecuniary penalty—fine; pecuniary interest—financial interest (in property).

Penal Code: A statute which lists and defines prohibited conduct (crimes) and the punishments associated with each.

Penalty: A punishment fixed by law, as for a crime or breach of contract.

Peremptory: Means demanding people do things your way and do them now or a final judgment or decision, especially one made by a court.

Perfection: The proper recording or filing of an instrument, thereby giving notice to the world; usually applied to the perfecting of a security interest under the Uniform Commercial Code.

Performance Bonds: Bonds or guarantees given to clients by specialist insurers, on behalf of contractors and at their expense, binding the insurers to compensate clients (up to the amount of the bond obtained) in the event of a default.

Performance Specifications: The initial document for the designing of a structure, industrial complex, or engineering device, such as an instrument, machine, or control system, or for conducting scientific research. The performance specifications contain feasibility reports for development, the basic specifications for the structure or article, and the initial data needed for design. They state the purpose of the project, the area of use, the development stages and composition of design documentation, and completion deadlines, as well as special requirements resulting from specific features of the project itself or the project's operating conditions. The performance specifications are usually drawn up on the basis of analysis of the results of preliminary research, calculations, and modeling.

Perjury: False swearing; a willful false statement given under oath in a judicial proceeding.

Perpetrator: Person who committed the offence.

Perpetual Succession: Ownership of property remains with a group or organization as a whole, not individual members of the group.

Personal Property: Things temporary or movable as distinguished from real property.

Petition: An application in writing for an order of the court.

Petition in Bankruptcy: An official document filed in a Federal court to have a debtor declared bankrupt.

Plaintiff: One who commences a court action against a defendant.

Pleadings: Formal allegations, either written or oral, make by the parties of a lawsuit stating their respective claims and defenses in the action.

Pledge: A deposit of personal property as a security for the performance of an act or satisfaction of an obligation and/or a promise.

Point of Law: An individual legal issue or proposition at the heart of a case.

Possessory Title: A possessory title means that the title is subject to any adverse interests which exist at the date of registration, *e.g.*, the claims of the true owner.

Postponement: The postponement of an event is the act of delaying it happening or arranging for it to take place at a later time than originally planned.

Power of Attorney: An instrument in writing authorizing another to act as agent on behalf of the person whose signature appears on the document.

Practical Completion: The completion of all the work that has to be done.

Precedent: The doctrine by which courts are obliged to follow past decisions or Court judgment which is cited as an authority in a later case involving similar facts. Precedent cannot bind a higher court (for example, a Circuit Court decision cannot bind a High Court judge). A Supreme Court judgment binds all courts – although it does not bind the Supreme Court itself in future cases. The system of precedent forms the basis of the policy of stare decisis which helps litigants to predict the outcome of a case in a given situation.

Preference: Paying or securing to one or more creditors, by an insolvent debtor, of all or a part of a claim to the exclusion of other creditors or special advantage given to someone.

Preferred Creditor: A preferential creditor (in some jurisdictions called a preferred creditor) is a creditor who receives a preferential right to payment upon the debtor's bankruptcy under applicable insolvency laws.

Pre-hearing Conference: An informal conference between the parties in a court action to try to reach a settlement or clarify any matters in dispute before the full hearing.

Preliminaries: That part of the bills of quantities which describes the works in general terms and lists the contractor's general obligations, the restrictions imposed by the employer and the contractual terms.

Premises: A building or part of a building usually including the adjacent grounds.

Prerogative Writ: A writ issued by a higher court (*e.g.*, the Supreme Court) to prevent lower courts and officials from exceeding their powers or to compel them to exercise their functions, *e.g.*, habeas corpus mandamus , certiorari.

Pre-sentence Report: A report, usually prepared by the Department of Human Services, for the court to consider before sentencing a young person.

Prescription: The method of acquiring an easement upon another's real property by continued and regular use without permission of the property owner for a period of years required by the law of the state.

Presumption: A conclusion or inference which may or must be drawn from other established facts. Presumptions are important in the law of evidence.

Price: The consideration in money given for the purchase of a thing.

Prima Facie: At first sight. A prima facie fact is one that seems to be correct, but may subsequently be proved wrong by other evidence.

Primary Point of Contact: For the funder, the individual who is responsible for enforcing the performance of the contract terms and conditions and serving as liaison with the contractor. The provider's primary point of contact is the employee delegated to serve as the provider's representative and liaison to the contract funder.

Prime Cost: The total of direct material costs, direct labor costs, and direct expenses.

Prime cost Sum: In a bill of quantities, the price placed against an item requiring the contractor to enter into a nominated subcontract. The expression is to be distinguished from other uses of the expression prime cost; the tenuous connection is that under the usual nomination system the main contractor is, in respect of that work, paid whatever he (the main contractor) must pay the nominated subcontractor.

Prime Contract: Contract held either by the owner of a project, or by a main or primary contractor having full responsibility for the job.

Principal: (*i*) In the context of an agency, the party on whose behalf the agent acts.

(*ii*) In the context of a guarantee, the party whose obligations are being guaranteed.

Priorities: Debts entitled to payment before general creditors in bankruptcy. Also, the right held by a creditor by virtue of a lien or security to be satisfied out of the debtor's assets before other creditors.

Privity of Contract: Only the parties to a contract can sue each other over breaches of contract.

Probate: Official processing of a will to prove its authenticity. Upon accepting the validity of a will, there is generally an administration of the estate to carry out the directions of the deceased, to discover and collect assets, to pay all proper claims and taxes and to make ultimate distribution to those entitled to it.

Probate Law: That part of the law which regulates wills and other subjects related to the distribution of a deceased person's estate.

Probation: A non-custodial sentencing order that involves good behavior and supervision by a probation officer under defined reporting conditions for a specified period.

Proceedings: A sequence of events occurring at a particular place or occasion.

Procure: To encourage or persuade someone to commit an offence.

Procurement: The acquisition of goods or services in exchange for money.

Programme: A diagrammatic representation of the intended sequence of building operations.

Prohibited Name: A name which cannot be registered because it is obscene or offensive, impracticable or against the public interest.

Prohibition: An order to stop decision-making proceedings in a lower court or tribunal.

Prohibition Notice: A notice banning a workplace activity that may risk safety or health of any person.

Project Program: A document setting forth project requirements, constraints, and design objectives including space requirements and relationships, needed flexibility and expandability, special equipment and systems, and site requirements.

Project Representative: The design professional's or Facility's representative at the project site who assists in the administration of the construction contract.

Prolongation: (*i*) Usually delay in the completion of the works that is the responsibility of the employer. (*ii*) Synonym for prolongation costs.

Prolongation Costs: Loss and expense caused to a contractor by reason of prolongation.

Promissory Note: A signed promise in writing to pay a specified sum at an expressed time on demand.

Proof: Evidence that establishes truth or falsehood of fact.

Proof of Claim: A claim form required to be filed with the court in the estate of a bankrupt (or similar proceedings), if a creditor is to receive payment (or its pro-rata share) of a debt owed.

Property: Anything which is the subject of ownership whether real or personal, tangible or intangible.

Proprietorship: Single ownership of a business.

Pro-Rata: A calculated proportionate share or sum.

Pro-Rate: Voluntary cash payment and distribution by a debtor of a uniform percentage.

Prosecution: The party presenting evidence against the person accused of committing a crime.

Pro Tanto: For so much. Means to the extent specified, but not more.

Protection Application: An application to a court by the Department of Human Services for intervention to protect the welfare of a child; may involve removal of the child from the family.

Pro Tempore (pro tem): For the time being.

Protest: A formal document declaring the dishonor of a negotiable instrument.

Provable Debt: A debt that must be accepted for proportional payment from available funds by the trustee of a bankrupt and from which the bankrupt is released on discharge from bankruptcy.

Provisional Sum: (*i*) An item in a bill of quantities designed to approximately estimate the cost of work yet to be particularized. (*ii*) The expression is sometimes loosely used to describe any approximate estimate of the cost of building work.

Proxy: A person who acts on behalf of another for a specific purpose, or the form used to make such an appointment. In a company a shareholder can appoint a proxy to attend a meeting and vote on their behalf.

Punch List: A list of items to be completed or corrected by the contractor before Substantial Completion can be established. The punch list is prepared by the Owner's Representative.

Punitive Damages: Special, exceptional damages ordered by a court where an act or omission was of a particularly serious, extensive or malicious nature. (Normally damages are awarded to compensate, not to punish).

Purchase Order: A purchase order (PO) is a commercial document issued by a buyer to a seller, indicating types, quantities, and agreed prices for products or services the seller will provide to the buyer. Sending a PO to a supplier constitutes a legal offer to buy products or services.

Pursuant to: According to, as directed by (an Act or Regulation).

Qq

Qualified Privilege: A defense in defamation actions that defeats the claim when the alleged defamation issues during specified occasions.

Qualified Title: A Land Registry title where there is a specified defect. Such a title has the same guarantee as absolute title – except for matters relevant to defect, which are not covered by the state guarantee.

Quality: The level of fitness for purpose which is specified for or achieved by any service, work or product.

Quality Assurance (QA): A discipline to assess quality standards, covering all activities and functions concerned with the attainment of quality.

Qualified Tender: A tender which does not fully meet the intended contractual requirements. Such tenders are not normally acceptable.

Quantum: [Latin: amount or extent.] An expression used to mean the amount of money a successful claimant will receive in a court action. Also used to refer to the assessment a lawyer (usually a barrister) will make which guides a claimant on whether his case is worth pursuing.

Quantum meruit: (Latin: as much as he has deserved) Principle stating that a person should not be obliged to pay (nor another allowed to receive) more than the value of the goods or services provided.

Quash: To overthrow; to make void or annul a court order; to cancel.

Quasi-Contract: A quasi contract is a contract that exists by order of a court, not by agreement of the parties. Courts create quasi contracts to avoid the unjust enrichment of a party in a dispute over payment for a good or service. In some cases a party who has suffered a loss in a business relationship may not be able to recover for the loss without evidence of a contract or some legally recognized agreement. To avoid this unjust result, courts create a fictitious agreement where no legally enforceable agreement exists.

Quasi-Delict: An act whereby a person, without malice, but by fault, negligence or imprudence not legally excusable, causes injury to another.

Quasi-Judicial: Administrative tribunals or government officials which, in their decision-making process, are subject to the rules of natural justice.

Queen's Bench: Originally, the common criminal court of the common law; later, the general superior court.

Queen's Counsel: An archaic designation of a barrister, phased out in most jurisdiction, indicating of its title holder faithfulness to the Crown, but more recently, contribution to the profession of lawyers.

Question of Discretion: Where an appeal predominantly takes issue with the lower court's exercise of judicial discretion.

Question of Fact: An issue that involves the resolution of a factual dispute or controversy and is within the sphere of the decisions to be made by a jury. A question of fact is a factual dispute between litigants that must be resolved by the jury at trial. It is an issue that is material to the outcome of the case and requires an interpretation of conflicting views on the factual circumstances surrounding the case.

Question of Law: Questions touching the scope, effect or application of a rule of law which the courts apply in determining the rights of parties.

Question of Privilege: A term of parliamentary law and procedure which refers to an urgent motion made at a meeting which seeks an immediate ruling on an alleged violation of the rights or privileges of members as a whole, or in regards to a negative personal remark.

Quid Pro Quo: The giving of one valuable thing for another, something given for something.

Quit: For a tenant to move out of rented premises.

Quitclaim: To release or relinquish claim or title to, especially in deeds to real property.

Quid Pro Quo: The mutual consideration that passes between two parties to a contractual agreement, thereby rendering the agreement valid and binding.

Quorum: The minimum number of people needed at a meeting for it to proceed and make any decisions.

Quotation: Any offer by a supplier to supply goods, works or services requested either orally or in writing. A quotation may be the written confirmation of an earlier offer.

Quo warranto: (Latin: by what authority) Judicial review procedure questioning the authority of a person or organization.

Rr

Rate Contract: A contract that establishes a rate of payment for a specified unit of service.

Ratification: Giving authority to an act that has already been done. A company general meeting resolution can ratify an act previously done by the directors, or a principal can choose to ratify the act of an agent that was beyond the specified power of the agent.

Ratify: To approve or confirm a contract or act performed by another.

Red Herring: An irrelevant legal issue.

Real Property: Land and everything that is permanently affixed to it.

Reasonable Wear and Tear: damage sustained in the course of normal use.

Rebuttal: Evidence introduced to counter, disprove or contradict the opposition's evidence or a presumption, or responsive legal argument.

Rebuttable Presumption: Presumed fact based on the proof of other facts. Most presumptions are rebuttable, which means that the person against whom the presumption applies may present evidence to the contrary, thus nullifying the presumption. If a person has not been heard of for seven years by people who should have seen him, he may be presumed dead – but this presumption is rebutted if he turns up!

Receiver: A person who is appointed by a court to receive, and hold in trust, property in litigation.

Receivership: The appointment of a licensed insolvency practitioner to take over the running of a company. A creditor with a secured debt appoints the receiver. The job of the receiver is to recover the debt either by taking the security and selling it or by running the business as a going concern until the debt is paid off (see liquidation).

Reciprocity: A term of international treaties by which two or more states agree to extend to the other's citizens specified legal rights on the same standing as its own citizens.

Recitals: Introductory paragraphs of a contract that describe the nature of the contract and why each party has elected to enter into the agreement.

Reclamation: A term used in bankruptcy to denote a right or proceeding on the part of a person having title to property to recover the same when it is in possession of the bankrupt, debtor, receiver or trustee.

Reconvention: A rule of jurisdiction which enables a counterclaim against another who, although otherwise beyond the jurisdiction of the court, has voluntarily submitted to jurisdiction by iniating the principal action.

Record: To place on file in official books. The recording of a judgment in the county of the judgment debtor becomes a lien on all the debtor's real property not exempt from execution.

Record Retention: The requirement to keep all client records, financial records, supporting documents, statistical records, and any other documents (including electronic storage media) pertinent to the contract for a period of five (5) years after termination of the contract, or if an audit has been initiated and audit findings have not been resolved at the end of five (5) years, he records shall be retained until resolution of the audit findings or any litigation which may be based on the terms of the contract.

Re-cross Examination: The resumption of cross-examination by the original cross-examiner in order to respond to matters that may have arisen during the re-examination of a witness.

Recuse: To disqualify oneself as a judge.

Reddendum: Latin: that part of a lease which sets out the amount of rent and when it is payable.

Redemption of Shares: Where a company issues shares on terms stating that they can be bought back by the company. Not all shares can be redeemed, only those stated to be redeemable when they were issued. The payment for the shares must generally come from reserves of profit so that the capital of the company is preserved.

Redact: To edit, revise.

Referee: A person to whom a cause pending in a court is referred by the court to take testimony, hear the parties, and report thereon to the court, or to make a judicial determination—the referee is an officer exercising judicial powers and is an arm of the court for a specific purpose

Refugee: A person who is outside his state of origin or of residence, and cannot return for fear of human-rights related persecution.

Registered Office: The official address of the company as stated on the register at Companies House. Any documents delivered to this address are considered to be legally served on the company.

Release: To relinquish or surrender a privilege, right or claim by one in favor of another.

Re-measurement Contract: Hybrid between lump-sum contract and cost contract.

Remedy/Remedies: Payments or actions ordered by the court as settlement of a dispute. The most common is damages (a payment of money). Others include specific performance (of an action required in the contract), injunction (see the general contract terms above) and rescission - putting things back to how they were before the contract was signed.

Remittance: When a debtor makes payment to the attorney, the attorney puts the money into his account to clear. After it has cleared, the attorney makes a remittance to the forwarder, which is less his commissions.

Remittitur: Legal process by which an appellate court transmits to the court below the proceedings before it, together with its decision, for such further action and entry of judgment as is required by the decision of the appellate court.

Reorganization (Under the Bankruptcy Act): Debtor reorganizes, rather than liquidates, and creditors claim future earnings of the bankrupt, rather than property presently held.

Request for Proposals (RFP): Is a written solicitation for competitive sealed proposals with the title, date, and hour of the public opening designated. RFPs include a statement of the services sought, contractual terms and conditions applicable to the services, proposal evaluation criteria, and specific instructions for submitting proposals.

Repeal: The annulment of an existing law by the enactment of a new law. If the new law declares the old law to be revoked, the repeal is express. If the new law has provisions that contradict the old law so that both cannot logically exist together, the new law takes precedence and the repeal is implied.

Replevin: An action by an attorney to recover property sold under contract when the purchaser refuses to surrender such goods voluntarily and is in default of the terms of the agreement.

Repossess: To take possession again of a property or goods after non-payment of money owed. This might follow a court order.

Repudiation: Have two meanings in contract law. The first is where a party refuses to comply with a contract and this amounts to a breach of contract. The second is where a contract was made by a minor (person under the age of 18) who then repudiates it at or shortly after the age of 18. Then the repudiation voids the contract rather than causing a breach of contract.

Res Judicata: A thing judicially acted upon or decided.

Rescind: To void or cancel an agreement or contract.

Respondent: One who formally answers the allegations stated in a petition which has been filed with the court. Also known as a defendant in a civil action.

Restore/ Reinstate to Calendar: To reinstate the action to active inventory.

Restrictive Covenant: Is often included in long-term contracts and contracts of employment to stop the parties working with competitors during the period of the agreement and for some time thereafter. However, unless carefully written the courts will see them as being a restraint of trade and not enforce them.

Retainer: A retainer is a sum of money paid in advance to retain the services of an attorney, and should be taken into account in determining the ultimate fee to be charged for services rendered and results obtained.

Retention: The money deducted and retained by the employer from sums that would otherwise be due to the contractor, usually 5 per cent. The retention fund is usually released as to half upon practical completion and as to the other half upon the architect's certificate of completion of making good defects.

Retroactive: Effective as of a past date.

Retrospective: Applying to circumstances existing before the date on which a law came into effect.

Retrospective Delay Analysis: At the process of analysing responsibility and lay on a project after that delay has occurred.

Return: The answer made by a Sheriff, or other officer, to the court stating what has been done to execute a writ previously issued.

Reversed: A term used by a higher court to indicate that the decision of the lower court has been set aside.

Revocation: Cancelling the effect of a previous act, *e.g.*, an earlier will.

Revoked: To recall, cancel or wipe out the legal effect of something.

Ss

Sale: Transfer of ownership and possession of property from one to another for a sum of money or for other consideration.

Salvage: Compensation paid by the owners for saving ships, aircraft and property from the sea.

Sanction: A penalty or punishment provided as a means of enforcing obedience to a law, rule or code; also, an authorization.

Satisfaction: The discharge of an obligation by paying a party what is due.

Satisfaction Guaranteed: A term in a sales or services contract in which the seller defers to the buyer the sole and unilateral discretion as to whether or not the goods or services tendered are acceptable. In the event the price is not paid, no cause of action exists unless the buyer acting in good faith is satisfied, no matter how good the goods or services are in terms of quality.

Satisfaction of Judgment: A document signed by a judgment creditor (the party owed the money judgment) stating that the full amount due on the judgment has been paid.

Schedules: Technically, the schedules of assets and liabilities; is also commonly used to include the statement of financial affairs.

Schedule of Rates: Lists of jobs, like those in bills of quantities except that they contain no quantities. Rates may be inserted by tenderers, or by clients. In the latter case, tenderers specify their overall percentages on or off these rates.

Seal: To close a case file from public scrutiny - in instances of youthful offenders and acquittal, sealing orders are issued by the court to prevent the public from obtaining information on the cases.

Search: An inspection carried out to establish whether any legal restraints, planning applications or aspects of legal ownership might affect the purchase of a property. Solicitors will look into land registry and local government records when pursuing this.

Search Warrant: A court order that gives a police the permission to enter private property and to search for evidence of the commission of a crime, for the proceeds of crime or property that the police suspect may be used to commit a crime.

Secured Claim: Where a claim is secured by a lien, the code limits that secured claim to the value of the property less any higher priority liens.

Secured Creditor: A creditor holding a lien (secured claim) on property.

Security: A guarantee, as applied to an obligation, such as a mortgage, given a debtor to insure the payment or performance of its debt.

Security Agreement: An agreement whereby assets of a buyer, or borrower, are pledged as security for a loan or extension of credit.

Security for Costs: An undertaking required by a court to cover the payment of costs if the judgment is against the depositor.

Security Interest: Any interest in property acquired by contract for the purpose of securing payment or performance of an obligation.

Seisin: The legal possession of property; historically, possession under claim of freehold.

Separation: In matrimonial law, a cessation of cohabitation of husband and wife by mutual agreement, or in the case of "judicial separation," under the decree of a court.

Sequester: To separate, set apart, hold aside for safekeeping or awaiting some determination; jurors are sequestered when not permitted to return home until the case is closed.

Service: The exhibition or delivery of a writ, notice, etc., officially notifying a person of some action or proceeding in which that person is concerned.

Service Contract: Directors and officers of a company are usually given service contracts that are different to an employment contract. This is because directors and officers are not always employees and the effect of employment law is different.

Setoff: A counter claim that a defendant has against a plaintiff and which arises out of a different transaction.

Settlement: This is when the debtor offers a sum of money or products to settle a debt.

Shareholders Agreement: An agreement between all of the shareholders about how the company should be run and the application of the rights of the shareholders. This acts as a contract between the shareholders. The company itself is not bound by it, as it is not a party to the agreement.

Sheriff: Individuals empowered to ensure the security of the courthouse generally and courtrooms especially, to keep prisoners secure whilst in the courthouse, to secure jurors during trials and to assist in the execution of court order.

Short form Order: Short form order refers to a form used by a judge directing that some action be taken.

Show Cause Order: An order from a court or judge to a litigant ordering him to appear at a stated time to give a good reason why a conditional order should not be made absolute or why something should not be permitted or done in the case.

Sine Die: Adjourned without giving any future date of meeting or hearing. A court that adjourns sine die essentially dismisses the case by saying that it never wants to hear the case again.

Skip: This is when the debtor leaves the area in which he incurred the debt and cannot be located.

Skip Tracing: A service and attorney uses in order to locate the debtor.

Solicitation: Act or instance of requesting or seeking bid, business, or information. Unlike an offer, a solicitation is not a clear indication of the intention to enter into a binding agreement.

Solicitation Document: A written, competitive procurement instrument.

Solicitation Opening Clerk: The individual charged with the responsibility of receiving, logging, and opening solicitation documents.

Solvent: An individual, partnership or corporation able to pay its legal debts as they become due (where assets exceed liabilities).

Special Master: A special master is an attorney appointed on an adhoc basis to assist the court in hearing motions.

Special Proceedings: General term for remedies or proceedings which are not ordinary actions, *e.g.*, condemnation.

Special Referee (Or referee): The special referee has the authority to exercise judicial functions when assigned duties by the court to determine the following (1) to determine an issue (binding) (2) to perform an act (disclosure) (3) to hear and report - matrimonial actions may be included.

Special Term: A court part set aside to hear specific types of cases.

Special Verdict: A special finding of the facts of a case by a jury leaving to the court the application of the law to the facts thus found.

Special Provision: A section of the Attachment I containing any special requirements not covered elsewhere in the contract.

Stamp Duty: A tax on legal documents, publications, etc., the payment of which is certified by the attaching or impressing of official stamps.

Statement of Need: A narrative describing the circumstances which contribute to the necessity for the project to exist.

Statement of Work: A narrative describing what services are to be provided, how the services are to be provided, measurable objectives, products to be delivered, and schedules of performance.

Statute of limitations: a statute that declares that no actions of a specified kind be commenced after a specified period of time after the cause of action arose.

Status Report: This is a regular report that the attorney must write to the forwarder informing him of each and every thing that is being done to collect the file.

Statute of Limitations: A law which limits the length of time within which a suit must be commenced before the right to sue is lost.

Statutory Lien: A lien arising under a statute, not including a security interest or judicial lien.

Stay: An order of the court to postpone a legal proceeding.

Stay: The act of temporarily stopping a judicial proceeding through the order of a court.

Stipulation: An agreement between attorneys that concerns business before a court and is designed to simplify or shorten litigation and save costs.

Stipulation of Settlement: A formal agreement between litigants and/or their attorneys resolving their dispute.

Sua sponte: (Sooh-uh spahn-tay) adj. Latin for "of one's own will," meaning on one's own volition, usually referring to a judge's order made without a request by any party to the case. These include an order transferring a case to another judge due to a conflict of interest or the judge's determination that his/her court does not have jurisdiction over the case.

Subcontract: A written contract between a contracted provider and another entity to deliver program services included within the provider's contract with its funder.

Sub-contracting: The process where a contractor assigns part of the contract to another contractor(s).

Sub-contractor: A company or an individual employed by the main contractor to perform a sub-contract.

Subject to contract: Words used on documents exchanged by parties during contract negotiations. They denote that the document is not an offer or acceptance and negotiations are ongoing. Often the expression 'without prejudice' is used when what is really meant it 'subject to contract'.

Sublease: A lease that is given by a tenant of part or all of the leased premises, to another person for a period shorter than the original lease, while still retaining some interest.

Subordination: An arrangement by which certain claims may not be paid before others. Subpoena—A writ or order directed to a person and requiring his or her attendance at a particular time and place, to testify as a witness.

Subpoena DucesTecum: An order not only for the purpose of compelling a witness to appear in court, but also requiring the witness to bring books and records which may be in his or her possession and which may tend to disclose information or explain the subject matter of the trial.

Subrogation: The substitution of one person in place of a creditor whose rights he acquires.

Subsequent Proceedings: Any proceeding or action taken with respect to a specific case after it has been filed with the court.

Substantial Completion: That degree of completion which is ordinarily necessary for the contractor to recover anything under a lump-sum contract. It is usually a lesser degree of completion than practical completion or entire completion.

Sue: To take legal action.

Suit: A legal action or proceeding.

Suit Fee: A suit fee is a fee payable to the receiver in addition to the commission, for legal services rendered by the receiver for the creditor involving court action in connection with the prosecution of a commercial claim. These monies may be made, in whole or part, contingent.

Suit Filed: This is when an attorney files a lawsuit in the local court to have the court rule on the validity of the claim.

Sum Certain: Liquidated damages pursuant to contract, promissory note, law, etc.

Summary Judgment: A remedy for having the court decides a case on affidavits and pleadings without the necessity of a full trial; usually granted when no trial able issue is presented.

Summary Offence: A minor offence heard and decided in a Magistrates' Court and not sent for trial before a judge and jury.

Summons: A writ or notice requiring a person to appear before a court to answer a complaint by a certain date.

Specification: The document which we use to set out our requirements for the goods or services.

Supplementary Proceedings: A statutory action and procedure requiring the debtor to answer, under oath, questions put by the creditor's attorney.

Surety: A person who agrees to be liable for the debt or contractual obligations of another.

Suspended Sentence: A sentence of imprisonment which is only served if the convicted person commits further offences. May be partially or wholly suspended, or a combined custody and treatment order.

Suspension: Exclusion of a student from school for a specified period as a disciplinary measure; less severe punishment than expulsion.

Sustainability: A process whereby organizations meet their needs for goods, services, works and utilities in a way that achieves value for money on a whole life basis in terms of generating benefits not only to the organization, but also to society and the economy, whilst minimizing damage to the environment".

Sworn Evidence: Evidence given under oath.

Tt

Take Down Notice: A notice sent to an Internet service provider alleging and detailing unlawful publishing activity.

Takeover Bid: An attempt to assume control or management of a corporation by another corporation, generally by purchase of all outstanding stock.

Tangible Property: Tangible property is property you own that can be touched and (usually) moved. Examples include stamps, jewelry, cars and artwork. Land is not considered tangible property.

Tax Avoidance: The lawful arrangement or planning of one's affairs so as to reduce liability to tax. Compare Tax Evasion.

Tax Evasion: Any illegal action taken to avoid the lawful assessment of taxes; for example, by concealing or failing to declare income. Compare Tax Avoidance.

Tender: Document submitted by an organization including business questionnaire, instructions to tenderers, contract conditions, specification, pricing document, form of tender and tenderers responses for the delivery of supplies, services or works in response to an invitation to tender. This normally involves submission of the offer in a sealed envelope to a specified address by a specified time and date.

Tender Documents: Documents provided to prospective tenderers when they are invited to tender and that form the basis on which tenders are submitted, including instructions to tenderers, contract conditions, specification, pricing document, form of tender and tenderers responses.

Tender Evaluation Panel: A group of people who analyse tenders received and make final recommendations on the award of contracts.

Tender Process: The official process of advertising a contract, inviting organizations to tender, evaluation of tender submissions and subsequent award of a contract.

Tenancy: The term is often used in a more restricted sense, however, for the arrangement in which the owner (the Landlord) allows another person (the tenant) to take possession of the land for an agreed period, usually in return for rent. There are many ways of establishing a tenancy, from a formal lease by deed to an informal verbal arrangement. The latter is legally binding on the parties if it satisfies the requirements for an agreement for a lease.

Tenancy in Common: Two or more persons who hold land or other property in common.

Tenendum: Latin: to be held. In law, that part of a contract in which an interest in real property is created that sets out the extent or limitations of that interest.

Tenure: A right, term, or mode of holding or occupying something of value for a period of time. In feudal law, the principal mode or system by which a person held land from a superior in exchange for the rendition of service and loyalty to the grantor. The status given to an educator who has satisfactorily completed teaching for a trial period and is, therefore, protected against summary dismissal by the employer. A length of time during which an individual has a right to occupy a public or private office.

Term Contract: An indefinite quantity contract wherein a party agrees to furnish commodities or contractual services during a prescribed period of time, the expiration of which concludes the contract.

Testamentary Capacity: The legal ability to sign a will.

Testimony: An oral declaration made by a witness or party under oath.

Theory of the Case: A short, succinct statement of the theme of an action as evidence will be presented organized and support at trial.

Third Party: A person who is not privy to a contract or a party in a lawsuit.

Third-party Action: A claim asserted by a defendant, styled a third-party plaintiff, against a person, styled a third-party defendant.

Third Party Claim: A demand made by a person (not a party to an action) for delivery or possession of personal property, title to which is claimed by the third party.

Time-Bar Clause: A clause in a contract which sets a strict deadline within which either party may bring a dispute to either a court or to arbitration.

Time of the Essence: A contractual term requiring performance within a specified time.

Title Deeds: The deeds and documents which provide evidence of a person's right or title to an interest in property. Nowadays, all such interests must be registered at the Land Registry following completion.

Tort: A wrongful act, other than a breach of contract, such that the law permits compensation of damages.

Total Aggregated Value: The total value of the overall requirement over the contract term. Individual or annual values are irrelevant where goods, services or works are of the same type or have similar characteristics.

Trade-mark: A registered name or logo that is protected by law. Trade-marks must be granted through the Patent Office.

Trade Secrets: The whole or any portion or phase of any formula, pattern, device, combination of devices, or compilation of information which is for use, or is used, in the operation of a business and which provides the business an advantage, or an opportunity to obtain an advantage, over those who do not know or use it.

Traditional Contracting: Contracting where the contractor is not responsible for design, and executes the work for a lump sum, which is usually subject to adjustment. Contrast design and build contracting and management contracting.

Traditional Indemnity: An indemnity which bites regardless of whether the indemnitor is to blame for the subject matter of the indemnity. Contrast comparative indemnity.

Transcript: The official record of proceedings in a trial or hearing.

Transfer: The removal of a cause from the jurisdiction of one court or judge to another by lawful authority.

Trespass: A willful act or active negligence that causes an injury to a person or the invasion of their property or unlawful interference with another person or his property or rights. Trespass is a civil, not a criminal, offence and is actionable without proof of any actual damage.

Trial: The formal examination of a legal controversy in court so as to determine the issue.

Trial Date: Once the lawsuit is filed, the court sets a trial date when the matter will be heard by a judge.

Trial De Novo: A new trial or retrial during which a whole case is retried as if no trial ever occurred in the first place.

Tribunal: A body set up to hear and decide disputes, usually with less formality and less strict rules of evidence than in a court proceeding.

Trust Account: A special bank account where lawyer deposits money held on behalf of other people, subject to strict accounting rules.

Trust Deed: A legal document that evidences an agreement of a borrower to transfer legal title to real property to an impartial third party, a trustee, for the benefit of a lender, as security for the borrower's debt. A trust deed, also called a deed of trust or a Potomac mortgage, is used in some states in place of a mortgage.

Trustee: The person who manages a trust, the trustee, has a legal duty to manage the trust's assets in the best interests of the beneficiary or beneficiaries. Typical trustee duties include managing rental properties, investing funds or paying income to the beneficiary.

Turnkey Contract: An expression sometimes used to describe a design and build contract where the contractor not only designs and builds the building but also designs and installs any plant necessary. The idea is that all the employer has to do is to turn the key to the front door and start using the building.

Turnover Proceeding: A hearing after a judgment has been issued, in which a creditor seeks to establish through evidence that the debtor (or a third party who is in possession of the debtor's property) is in possession of money or property that would satisfy, or partially satisfy, the judgment.

Uu

Uberrima Fides: A legal principle in which all parties to a contract must make full disclosure of material facts in order for the contract to be effective. It is used in insurance contracts, in which the potential policyholder must declare all illnesses, injuries or other facts that would change the policy's level of risk. The phrase "uberrima fides" is Latin for "utmost good faith".

Ultra Vires: Beyond one's powers. If an organisation does something ultra vires, what it has done is invalid.

Umpire: Another word for an arbitrator or an arbitrator appointed to resolve arbitration when the original arbitrators cannot agree.

Unascertained Goods: Goods that are not specifically identified at the time a contract of sale is made. For example, in a contract for the sale of 1000 tons of soya bean meal, the seller may deliver any 1000 tonnes that answer the contract description. When the correct quantity has been set aside for delivery to the buyer, the goods are described as ascertained. Ownership does not pass to the buyer until the goods have been ascertained.

Unbundled Legal Services: A practice in which the lawyer and client agree that the lawyer will provide some, but not all, of the work involved in traditional full service representation. Simply put, the lawyers perform only the agreed upon tasks, rather than the whole "bundle," and the clients perform the remaining tasks on their own.

Under Lease: The lease of a property by a tenant of the property to someone else.

Under Protest: A qualification made to a legal action taken by a person that the action is contrary to the intent or desire of the person making the protest.

Undertaking: A promise, especially in legal proceedings, that creates an obligation. A solicitor who breaks such a promise will be in breach of disciplinary that can be taken as evidencing the existence of the contract.

Underwriter: A person who signs as party to a contract. Now usually only applied to insurance contracts where the underwriters are those who agree to bear all or part of the risk in return for the premium payments.

Undue Influence: Taking unfair or improper advantage of the weakness of another party to make them agree to something.

Unenforceable Contract: A contract that, although valid, cannot be enforced by action because it is neither evidenced in writing nor (when this is a permissible alternative) supported by a sufficient act of *part performance.

Unfair Prejudice: Unfair conduct on the part of those entrusted to run and control a company in respect of (usually minority) company members. Any member affected may apply to the court under the Companies Act 1985, and the court is empowered under the Act to make such order as it thinks fit. Commonly, the unfair conduct consists of actions having the effect of seriously diminishing the value of the complainant's shareholding. In this instance the usual remedy sought is for the purchase of the complainant's shares at a fair price.

Unfair Terms: Some terms are made unfair by legislation and will not be enforced by the courts and may even be interpreted against the person who included them in the contract. The legislation mainly protects consumers, but can also apply where there is a business-to-business contract in which one party is significantly more powerful than the other.

Union: A defined group of employees formed for the purposes of representing those employees with the employer as to the terms of a collective contract of employment.

Unit Trust: A trust which manages investments. People can invest in unit trusts by buying units. The managers of the trust use the money people invest to buy investments. The fund manager values the fund's assets from time to time and puts a new price on the fund's units.

Unsecured Claim: A pre-petition claim which is not a priority claim and is not a secured claim is an unsecured claim.

Unsecured Creditor: Someone who has lent money without getting any security for the loan.

Unfair Terms: Some terms are made unfair by legislation and will not be enforced by the courts and may even be interpreted against the person who included them in the contract. The legislation mainly protects consumers, but can also apply where there is a business-to-business contract in which one party is significantly more powerful than the other.

Un Liquidated: The amount of damages decided by a court because the parties to a contract had not agreed in advance how much the damages would be for breaking the terms of the contract.

Usury: Charging an illegal rate of interest; unlawful interest in excess of the rate established by law.

Uterine: Describes people who have the same mother but different fathers.

Vv

Vacant Possession: The exclusive use of land, to which a purchaser is entitled on completion of the transaction unless he has contracted to buy subject to another's right of occupation.

Value Added Tax: A value added tax (VAT) is a form of consumption tax. It is a tax on the estimated market value added to a product or material at each stage of its manufacture or distribution, ultimately passed on to the consumer. It differs from a sales tax, which is levied only at the point of purchase.

Value for Money: The provision of the right goods and services from the right source, of the right quality, at the right time, delivered to the right place and at the right price (judged on whole life costs and not simply initial costs).

Variation: Any alteration, modification, addition to or deletion of any requirement of the contract terms or specification.

Variants: Tenders that meet minimum specifications but vary in technical terms. May be allowed by a contracting authority where award criterion is that of most economically advantageous tender.

Vendee: A person who buys something.

Vendor: A person who sells or offers to sell commodities or contractual services.

Venire: Is a legal term referring both to a writ ordering the assembly of a pool of prospective jurors, and to the pool of jurors itself.

Venue: The place where an action is tried, generally based on locality or judicial district, in which an injury occurred or a material fact happened, or where defendant resides.

Verdict: The formal decision or finding of a judge or jury.

Verification: An affidavit, under oath, swearing that writing is true.

Vested Interest: An established right that cannot be eliminated, as to some future benefit or close involvement in promoting personal advantage or a number of groups cooperating or competing in pursuing selfish goals and exerting controlling influence, esp. the powerful persons and groups that own and control industry, business, etc.

Vesting Order: A way the High Court transfers land without the need for a conveyance.

Vexatious Litigant: A person who regularly brings court cases which have little chance of succeeding.

Vicarious Liability: A situation where someone becomes responsible under the law for wrongs done by someone else. This often happens when an employee does something wrong while at work which becomes the employer's responsibility (such as an employee working negligently and causing someone else to be hurt because of the negligence).

Videlicet: (Latin: that is to say) The abbreviation of videlicet (*viz.*) is commonly used in legal documents to advise that what follows provides more detail about a preceding general statement.

Void: A void contract is one that cannot be performed or completed at all. A void contract is void from the beginning and the normal remedy, if possible, is to put things back to where they were before the contract. Contracts are void where one party lacks the capacity to perform the contracted task, it is based on a mistake, or it is illegal.

Voidable: The law distinguishes between void and voidable contracts. Some contracts have such a fundamental defect that they are said to be void. Others have more minor defects and are voidable at the option of the innocent party.

Voire Dire: (French: To speak the truth) Separate trial within a trial, generally in the absence of the jury, on the admissibility of contested evidence.

Volenti Non Fit Injuria: (Latin: those who consent may not be injured) Defense in tort which prevents a person who knowingly and voluntarily assumes a risk (by, for example, engaging in a dangerous sport) from later seeking compensation for any injury suffered.

Ww

Waiver: The intentional or voluntary yielding or relinquishment of a known legal claim, right or privilege. Warrant—A writ issued by a judge or competent authority, directing a Sheriff or officer to make an arrest or search.

Waqf: Muslim law: property dedicated to charitable purposes.

Ward of Court: A person who is protected by the High Court, such as a minor.

Warrant: An order in writing from a competent authority instructing that a certain act be carried out or In commercial and property law, a warrant also refers to a guarantee that a property being sold or transferred meets certain specified criteria.

Warranties: Promises made in a contract, but which are less than a condition. Failure of a warranty results in liability to pay but will not be a breach of contract unlike failure of a condition, which does breach the contract.

Warranty: In business and legal transactions, a warranty is an assurance by one party to the other party that specific facts or conditions are true or will happen; the other party is permitted to rely on that assurance and seek some type of remedy if it is not true or followed.

Watered Stock: Shares in a corporation which is stated to be, or issued as fully paid but which in fact, has not been paid for.

Wayleave: A right of way through or over a piece of land often for a particular purpose, such as for a pipeline to go through a piece of land or for goods to be carried over it.

Wharf: Under the Merchant Shipping Act 1894, any premises (including quays and docks) in or upon which goods landed from ships may be lawfully placed.

Whole Life Costing (WLC): Whole Life Costing means to take into consideration costs which incur at the start to the end of a product or a services lifecycle. These are design costs, acquisition costs, operating costs and disposal costs.

Whistleblower: Person who makes a complaint about illegal or inappropriate actions of their employer.

Without Prejudice: When written on a document, the document cannot be used as evidence that a contract or agreement exists.

Will: A will or testament is a legal declaration by which a person, the testator, names one or more persons to manage his/her estate and provides for the transfer of his/her property at death. For the devolution of property not disposed of by will, see inheritance and intestacy.

Winding up: Winding is the process by which the normal activities of the corporation or association of person is stopped and the assets and liabilities of the association is assessed and distributed among the shareholders as per the existing agreement.

Witness: The common definition of this word is a person who perceives an event (by seeing, hearing, smelling or other sensory perception). The legal definition refers to the court supervised recital of that sensory experience, in writing (deposition) or verbally (testimony).

Words of Art: Words which have a fixed meaning in law so that their use in a legal document can have only one interpretation.

Wound up: Winding-up is the formal procedure for disbanding a company.

Wounding with Intent: The aggravated assault of a person with the intention of causing *grievous bodily harm (even if grievous harm does not in fact result) or wounding with the intention of resisting a lawful arrest. Wounding with intent carries a maximum sentence of life imprisonment; a second conviction for wounding with intent to do grievous bodily harm carries a mandatory life sentence.

Wreck (Shipwreck): The destruction of a ship at sea, as by foundering in a storm or being driven onto rocks or the remains of a wrecked ship or goods cast up by the sea from a wrecked ship.

Writ: An order issued from a court in the name of the sovereign or state directing the person named to comply with the directions contained therein.

Writ of Delivery: Writ of execution to enforce a judgment for delivery of goods. It directs the *sheriff to seize the goods and deliver them to the claimant or to recover their assessed value. If the writ does not offer the defendant the option of retaining the goods by paying their assessed value, it is known as a writ of specific delivery.

Writ of Execution: A writ used in the *enforcement of a judgment. It may be a writ of *fierifacias, a *writ of possession, a *writ of delivery, a writ of *sequestration, or any further writ in aid of any of these writs.

Writ of Possession: A writ directing the *sheriff to enter upon land to give vacant possession to the claimant. It is used to enforce judgments for the possession of land.

Writ of Summons: Formerly, a writ by which an action was commenced in the High Court. Civil proceedings in the High Court are now initiated through a claim form.

Written off: The elimination of an asset or amount due from the books.

Wrongful: An act or omission that exposes a person to civil or criminal liability.

Wrongful Birth: A mother's claim in tort that she would not to have given birth to the child with serious genetic defects but for the defendant's negligence in testing or counseling.

Wrongful Conviction: A conviction of a person accused of a crime which, in the result of subsequent investigation, proves erroneous.

Wrongful Death: A law action which claims damages from any person who, through negligence or direct act or omission, caused the death of certain relatives (*e.g.*, spouse, children or parent).

Wrongful Trading: Continuing to trade while knowing that there is little prospect of the company being able to pay its debts.

Xx

X: A form of signature upon contracts

Xoanon: Primitive, usually wooden image of deity supposed to have fallen from Heaven; seldom found in Irish courtrooms.

Yy

Year-and-a-day Rule: A common law rule precluding prosecution for murder where the victim died a year and a day, or later, after the infliction of the ultimately fatal wounds.

Yellow Dog Contract: A name given in American labor law to contact of employment by which the employee promises not to join a union or agrees to forfeit employment if he / she joins a union during the period of employment.

York-Antwerp Rules: A set of internationally-accepted rules, first published in 1890, proposing points of detail in the application of the maritime law principle of general average.

Young Offender: A person between the ages of 14 and 17 who has committed a crime.

Your Honor: The proper way to address a judge in court.

Zz

Zealous Witness: A witness who displays undue favoritism towards one party in the case.

Zebra Crossing: A road crossing for pedestrians, identified by studs and alternating black and white stripes on the carriageway and lighted yellow globes(normally flashing) at each end. Pedestrians take precedence over vehicles on crossings uncontrolled by police or traffic wardens, and it is an offence for vehicles to wait or overtake within their limits.

Zero-rated Supply: A supply that is within the scope of value-added tax but is charged at a nil rate. Examples are food (excluding restaurant and take-away meals),books and journals, and children's clothes; all exports are also zero-rated. Unlike exempt supplies, zero-rated supplies count towards the turnover limit above which registration for VAT is compulsory, and any input tax relating to them may be reclaimed by the registered trader.

Zone or Zoning: The application of a law which restricts specified territory as to use.

Chapter 7

Acronyms—Alphabatically

AAB:	As Amended By
AAF:	Aggravation and Frustration
AAL:	Attorney At Law
A.C:	Law Reports Appeal Cases
ACO:	Administrative Contracting Officer
ACPM:	Associate Contractor Program Manager
ACPO:	Associate Contractor Project Office
ADCR:	Applicable Document Contractual Record
APO:	Automated Purchase Order
B.B:	Bail Bond
BOC:	Base Operations Contract
Bus. L.R:	Business Law Review
CA:	Contract Advice
CA:	Contract Award
CAL:	Contract Advice Letter
CAP:	Contractor-Acquired Property
CAR:	Contractual Action Request
CAS:	Contract Administrative Services
C.B:	Common Bench
CBB:	Contract Budget Baseline
CC:	Contract Completion

CCA:	Contract Change Authority/Authorization
CCN:	Contract Change Notification
CCN:	Contract Change Notice
CCN:	Contract Change Negotiation
CCO:	Customer Contracting Officer
CCP:	Contract Change Proposal
CCR:	Contractor Change Review
CCR:	Contract Change Record
CCR:	Contract Change Request
CCS:	Contract Control System
CDI:	Contract Definition Instruction
CDID:	Contract Data Item Description
CDMS:	Contractor Data Management System
CDR:	Contract Data Requirements
CDRL:	Contract Data Requirements List
CDRR:	Contract Documentation Requirements Record
CDRS:	Contract Data Requirements Schedule
CDSR:	Contract Data Status Report
CEI:	Contract End Item
CEIS:	Contract End Item Specification
CFSR:	Contract Fund Status Report/Review
CI:	Contract Initiation
C.I.F:	The total of cost, insurance and freight charges to be paid on goods purchased and shipped
CIS:	Contractor's Information Submittal
CLIN:	Contract Line Item Number
CMAO:	Contract Management Assistance Officer
CMN:	Contract Master Network
CMR:	Contractor Management Review
CMS:	Contract Master Schedule
CO:	Contracting Officer
COI:	Conflict of Interest
COR:	Contracting Officer Representative
COTR:	Contracting Officer's Technical Representative
CPM:	Contract Performance Management
CPO:	Conditional Purchase Offer

CPSR:	Contractor's Procurement System Review
CPR:	The Civil Procedure Rules
CR:	Contractor's Response
CRN:	Contract Revision Number
CSA:	Contractor Support Area
CSA:	Contract Specification Amendment
CSD:	Contract Start Date
Csl:	Counsel
CSR:	Contract Status Report
CTCI:	Contract Technical Compliance Inspection
CTM:	Contract Technical Manager
CTR:	Contract Technical Representative
CWBS:	Contract Work Breakdown Structure
DAB:	Dispute Adjudication Board
DAC:	Days after Contract
DCR:	Disposition of Contract Request
DESCA:	Development of a Simplified Consortium Agreement
DP:	Delayed Procurement
EOC:	End of Contract
EOPR:	Engineering Order Purchase Requisition
EOPR:	Engineering Order Purchase Request
EOT:	Extension of Time
EPC:	Engineering Procurement and Construction
EPR:	Engineering Purchase Request
ESSC:	Engineering Support Services Contract
FCCP:	Firm Contract Cost Proposal
FPC:	Fixed-Price Contract
HCJ:	High Court Judge
ICC:	International Chamber of Commerce
IPCA:	Integrated Projects Consortium Agreement
JHO:	Judicial Hearing Officer
J.R:	Judicial Review
L&AD:	Liquidated and Ascertained Damages
MIPR:	Military Intergovernmental Purchase Request
MPR:	Mock-up Purchase Request
MSA:	Major Subcontract Administrator

NAEB:	National Association of Educational Buyers
NAEP:	National Association of Educational Procurement
OCC:	Office of Contract Compliance
OFCC:	Office of Federal Contract Compliance
OFCCP:	Office of Federal Contract Compliance Programs
O.J.L.S:	Oxford Journal of Legal Studies
OR:	Official Referee
ORBA:	The Official Referees Bar Association
ORSA:	The Official Referees Solicitors Association
P&C:	Procurement and Contracts
P&SM:	Procurement and Subcontract Management
PCCN:	Provisioning Contract Control Number
PCCP:	Preliminary Contract Change Proposal
PCO:	Principal Contracting Officer
PCO:	Procuring Contracting Officer
PFI:	Private Finance Initiative.
PFP:	The Private Finance Panel
PN:	Professional Negligence
PO:	Purchase Order
POC:	Purchase Order Closeout
POCN:	Purchase Order Change Notice
POR:	Purchase Order Request
PQA:	Procurement Quality Assurance
PQC:	Procurement Quality Control
PQE:	Procurement Quality Engineering
PR:	Purchase Request
PR:	Procurement Regulation
PRD:	Procurement Regulation Directive
PRD:	Procurement Requirements Document
PSPL:	Priced Spare Parts List
PTR:	Pre Trial Review
QB:	Queen's Bench
QC:	Queen's Counsel
QV:	Abbreviation of good vide; for which see cross-reference
RIBA:	Royal Institute of British Architects
RPC:	Rules of professional conduct

SCA: Service Contract Act
SCJ: Senior Circuit Judge
SCL: Society of Construction Law
SCMP: System Contractor Management Plan
SDRL: Subcontract(or) Data Requirements List
SEM: Subcontractor Engineering Memorandum
SM: Subcontract Management
SMM: Subcontract Management Manual
SPR: Subcontractor Performance Review
SQA: Subcontractor Quality Assurance
SRR: Subcontractor Readiness Review
UNCITRAL: United Nations Commission on International Trade Law
TCC: Technology and Construction Court
TECBAR: The Technology and Construction bar Association.
TeCSA: The Technology and Construction Solicitors' Association.
TCL: Through Life Cost
Tr.L: Trading Law
V.A.T.T.R: Value Added Tax Tribunal Reports
WSF: Witness Statement of Fact
Y.B.W.A: Yearbook of World Affairs
Y.E.L: Yearbook of European Law

REFERENCES

- Oxford Dictionary of Law
- Building Contract Dictionary by David Chappell
- Project Management Terms Dictionary by Syed Ali Dilawer
- Law for Dummies by John Ventura
- Dictionary of Legal terms Steven H. Gifis
- Dictionary of Law by Elizabeth A Martin and Jonathan Law
- Black's Law Dictionary by Bryan Garner
- Contract Law by Adam Kramer
- Construction Contract Dictionary by Leonard Fletcher
- Engineering Contract Dictionary by Vincent Powell
- www.fidic.org
- www.jctcontracts.com
- Law of Contract: And The long man Dictionary Law L.B. Curzor , Paul Richards
- Contract Strategy for Successful Project Management by APM
- Hand-Book for Project Professionals by Syed Ali Dilawer
- A Practical and Easy reference guide for Specialist contractor by Rudi Klein, Barrister
- Practical Approach to Legal Advice and Drafting by Susan Blake
- Basic Contract Administration by Federal Acquisition Institute